The Word of the Buddha

An Outline of the Teachings
of the Buddha
in the Words of the Pāli Canon

Compiled, translated,
and explained by

Nyanatiloka Mahāthera

Buddhist Publication Society
Kandy • Sri Lanka

Buddhist Publication Society
P.O. Box 61
54, Sangharaja Mawatha
Kandy, Sri Lanka

Reprinted in 1981, 2001, 2011, 2015, 2019, 2024

National Library of Sri Lanka –
Cataloguing–in–Publication Data

Nyanatiloka himi

The Word of the Buddha : an outline of the teachings of the Buddha in the words of the Pali canon / Nyanatiloka himi – Kandy : Buddhist Publication Society, 2001
x, 94p. ; 21 cm.

ISBN 978-955–24–0364–4

i. 294.38 DDC 21 ii. Title

1. Buddhism – Sources

ISBN 978-955–24–0364–4

Typeset at the BPS

Printed in Sri Lanka by
Anura Printers (Pvt) Ltd.,
246, Kandy Road, Kurunegala.

Contents

Preface v

Abbreviations vii

The Pronunciation of Pāli viii

Introduction 1

The Four Noble Truths 5

I. The Noble Truth of Suffering 7

II. The Noble Truth of the Origin of Suffering 20

III. The Noble Truth of the Extinction of Suffering 26

IV. The Noble Truth of the Path that Leads to the Extinction of Suffering 30

1. Right Understanding 33
2. Right Thought 51
3. Right Speech 53
4. Right Action 56
5. Right Livelihood 58
6. Right Effort 60
7. Right Mindfulness 64
8. Right Concentration 80

Gradual Development of the Eightfold Path in the Progress of the Disciple 85

Preface
to the Eleventh Edition

The Word of the Buddha, published originally in German, was the first strictly systematic exposition of all the main tenets of the Buddha's teachings presented in the Master's own words as found in the *Sutta Piṭaka* of the Buddhist Pāli Canon.

While it may well serve as a first introduction for the beginner, its chief aim is to give the reader who is already more or less acquainted with the fundamental ideas of Buddhism, a clear, concise, and authentic summary of its various doctrines, within the framework of the all-embracing Four Noble Truths, i.e., the truths of suffering (inherent in all existence), its origin, its extinction, and the way leading to its extinction. From the book itself it will be seen how the teachings of the Buddha all ultimately converge upon the one final goal: deliverance from suffering. It was for this reason that on the title page of the first German edition there was printed the passage from the Aṅguttara Nikāya which says:

> Not only the fact of suffering do I teach,
> but also deliverance from it.

The texts, translated from the original Pāli, have been selected from the five great collections of discourses which form the Sutta Piṭaka. They have been grouped and explained in such a manner as to form one connected whole. Thus the collection, originally compiled for the author's own guidance and orientation in the many voluminous books of the Sutta Piṭaka, will prove a reliable guide for students of Buddhism. It should relieve them from the necessity of working their way through all these manifold Pāli scriptures, enabling them to acquire a comprehensive and clear view of the whole; and it should help them to relate to the main body of the doctrine the many details they will encounter in subsequent studies.

As the book contains many definitions and explanations of important doctrinal terms together with their Pāli equivalents, it can serve as a book of reference and a helpful companion throughout one's study of the Buddha's doctrine.

After the first German edition appeared in 1906, the first English version was published in 1907, and this has since run to ten editions, including an abridged students' edition (Colombo: YMBA, 1948) and an American edition (Santa Barbara, California: J.F. Rowny Press, 1950). It has also been included in Dwight Goddard's *Buddhist Bible*, published in the United States.

Besides subsequent German editions, translations have been published in French, Italian, Czech, Finnish, Russian, Japanese, Hindi, Bengali, and Sinhalese. The original Pāli of the translated passages was published in Sinhalese characters (edited by the author, under the title *Sacca-Saṅgaha*, Colombo, 1914) and Devanāgarī script in India.

The eleventh edition has been revised throughout. Additions have been made to the Introduction and to the explanatory notes, and some texts have been added.

NYANATILOKA

Abbreviations

DN	Dīgha Nikāya (the number refers to the sutta)
MN	Majjhima Nikāya (the number refers to the sutta)
AN	Aṅguttara Nikāya (the first number refers to the main division into parts or *nipātas*; the second number to the sutta)
SN	Saṃyutta Nikāya (the first number refers to the division into groups or *saṃyuttas*, the second number to the sutta)
Dhp	Dhammapada (by verse)
Ud	Udāna (by chapter and sutta)
Sn	Suttanipāta (by verse)
Vism	Visuddhimagga (*The Path of Purification*) (by chapter and section)
B. Dict.	*Buddhist Dictionary*, by Nyanatiloka Mahāthera
Fund.	*Fundamentals of Buddhism*, by Nyanatiloka Mahāthera

The Pronunciation of Pāli

THE VOWELS

a as 'u' in *cut*
ā as in *father*; never as in *take*
e is pronounced long as 'a' in *take*
i as in *pin*
ī as in *keen*; never as in *fine*
o is long as in *hope*
u as in *put*
ū as 'oo' in *boot*

THE CONSONANTS

c as 'ch' in *chair*
g as in *get*
h following consonants is always pronounced with a slight outward puff of breath
j as in *joy*
ṃ the so-called "nasalizer" is usually pronounced as 'ng' in *sung, sing,* etc.
s always as in *this*; never as in *these*
ñ as 'ny' in *canyon*
ph as in *haphazard*; never as in *photograph*
th as in *Thomas*; never as in *thin*
ṭ,ṭh, ḍ, ḍh are lingual sounds; in pronouncing, the tongue is to be pressed against the palate
Double consonants: each of them is to be pronounced;

e.g., *bb* as in *scrub-board*: *tt* as in *cat-tail.*

Introduction

1. *Buddha* or Enlightened One—lit. Knower or Awakened One—is the honorific name given to the Indian sage, Gotama, who discovered and proclaimed to the world the law of deliverance, known to the West by the name of Buddhism.

He was born in the sixth century B.C. at Kapilavatthu, as the son of the king who ruled the Sakya country, a principality situated in the border area of modern Nepal. His personal name was Siddhattha, and his clan name Gotama (Sanskrit: Gautama). In his twenty-nineth year he renounced the splendour of his princely life and his royal career, and became a homeless ascetic in order to find a way out of what he had early recognized as a world of suffering. After a six years' quest, spent under various teachers and in a period of fruitless self-mortification, he finally attained to Perfect Enlightenment (*sammā-sambodhi*), under the Bodhi tree at Gayā (today Bodh-Gayā). Forty-five years of tireless preaching and teaching followed and at last, in his eightieth year, there passed away at Kusinara that "undeluded being that appeared for the blessing and happiness of the world."

The Buddha is neither a god nor a prophet nor incarnation of a god, but a supreme human being who, through his own effort, attained to final deliverance and perfect wisdom, and became "the peerless teacher of gods and men." He is a "saviour" only in the sense that he shows people how to save themselves, by actually following to the end the path trodden and shown by him. In the consummate harmony of wisdom and compassion attained by the Buddha, he embodies the universal and timeless ideal of Man Perfected.

2. The *Dhamma* is the Teaching of Deliverance in its entirety, as discovered, realized, and proclaimed by the Buddha. It has been handed down in the ancient Pāli language, and preserved in three great collections of books, called *Tipiṭaka*, the "Three Baskets," namely: (I) the *Vinaya Piṭaka*, or Collection of Discipline, containing the rules of the monastic order; (II) the *Sutta Piṭaka*, or Collection of Discourses, consisting of various books of discourses, dialogues, verses, stories, etc., and dealing with the doctrine proper as summarized in the Four Noble Truths; (III) the *Abhidhamma Piṭaka*, or Philosophical Collection, presenting the teachings of the *Sutta Piṭaka*, in strictly systematic and philosophical form.

The Dhamma is not a doctrine of revelation, but the teaching of Enlightenment based on the clear comprehension of actuality. It is the teaching of the Fourfold Truth dealing with the fundamental facts of life and with liberation attainable through man's own effort towards purification and insight. The Dhamma offers a lofty but realistic system of ethics, a penetrative analysis of life, a profound philosophy, practical methods of mind training—in brief, all-comprehensive and perfect guidance on the path to deliverance. By answering the claims of both heart and reason, and by pointing out the liberating Middle Path that leads beyond all futile and destructive extremes in thought and conduct, the Dhamma has, and will always have, a timeless and universal appeal wherever there are hearts and minds mature enough to appreciate its message.

3. The *Sangha*—lit. the assembly, or community—is the Order of Bhikkhus or Mendicant Monks, founded by the Buddha and still existing in its original form in Burma, Thailand, Sri Lanka, Cambodia, Laos and Chittagong (Bengal). It is, together with the Order of the Jain monks, the oldest monastic order in the world. Amongst the most famous

disciples in the time of the Buddha were: Sāriputta who, after the Master himself, possessed the profoundest insight into the Dhamma; Moggallāna, who had the greatest supernatural powers; Ānanda, the devoted disciple and constant companion of the Buddha; Mahā-Kassapa, the president of the council held at Rājagaha immediately after the Buddha's death; Anuruddha, of divine vision and master of right mindfulness; and Rāhula, the Buddha's own son.

The Sangha provides the outer framework and the favourable conditions for all those who earnestly desire to devote their life entirely to the realization of the highest goal of deliverance, unhindered by worldly distractions. Thus the Sangha, too, is of universal and timeless significance wherever religious development reaches maturity.

The Threefold Refuge

The Buddha, the Dhamma, and the Sangha are called "The Three Jewels" (*tiratana*) on account of their matchless purity, and as being to the Buddhist the most precious objects in the world. These "Three Jewels" form also the "Threefold Refuge" (*tisaraṇa*) of the Buddhist, in the words by which he professes, or re-affirms, his acceptance of them as the guides of his life and thought.

The Pāli formula of refuge is still the same as in the Buddha's time:

Buddhaṃ saraṇaṃ gacchāmi.
Dhammaṃ saraṇaṃ gacchāmi.
Sanghaṃ saraṇaṃ gacchāmi.

I go for refuge to the Buddha.
I go for refuge to the Dhamma.
I go for refuge to the Sangha.

It is through the simple act of reciting this formula three times that one declares oneself a Buddhist. At the second and third repetition the words *dutiyampi* and *tatiyampi* ("for the second/third time") respectively are added before each sentence

The Five Precepts

After the formula of the Threefold Refuge usually follows the acceptance of the Five Moral Precepts (*pañca-sīla*). Their observance is the minimum standard needed to form the basis of a decent life and of further progress towards deliverance.

1. *Pāṇātipātā veramaṇī sikkhāpadaṃ samādiyāmi.*

   I undertake to observe the precept to abstain from killing living beings.

2. *Adinnādānā veramaṇī sikkhāpadaṃ samādiyāmi.*

   I undertake to observe the precept to abstain from taking things not given.

3. *Kāmesu micchācārā veramanī sikkhāpadaṃ samādiyāmi.*

   I undertake to observe the precept to abstain from sexual misconduct.

4. *Musāvādā veramaṇī sikkhāpadaṃ samādiyāmi.*

   I undertake to observe the precept to abstain from false speech.

5. *Surāmeraya–majja–pamādaṭṭhānā veramaṇī sikkhā–padaṃ samādiyāmi.*

   I undertake to observe the precept to abstain from intoxicating drinks and drugs causing heedlessness.

The Word of the Buddha

OR

The Four Noble Truths

Thus has it been said by the Buddha, the Enlightened One:

It is through not understanding, not realizing four things, that I, disciples, as well as you, had to wander so long through this round of rebirths. And what are these four things? They are:

> The noble truth of suffering (*dukkha*).
>
> The noble truth of the origin of suffering (*dukkha-samudaya*).
>
> The noble truth of the extinction of suffering (*dukkha-nirodha*).
>
> The noble truth of the path that leads to the extinction of suffering (*dukkha-nirodha-gāmini-paṭipadā*). (DN 16)

As long as the absolutely true knowledge and insight as regards these Four Noble Truths was not quite clear in me, so long was I not sure that I had won that supreme enlightenment which is unsurpassed in all the world with its heavenly beings, evil spirits, and gods, amongst all the hosts of ascetics and priests, heavenly beings and men. But as soon as the absolute true knowledge and insight as regards these Four Noble Truths had become perfectly clear in me, there arose in me the assurance that I had won that supreme unsurpassed enlightenment. (SN 56:11)

And I discovered that profound truth, so difficult to perceive, difficult to understand, tranquillizing and sublime, which is not to be gained by mere reasoning, and is visible only to the wise.

The world, however, is given to pleasure, delighted with pleasure, enchanted with pleasure. Truly, such beings will hardly understand the law of conditionality, the dependent origination (*paṭicca-samuppāda*) of everything; incomprehensible to them will also be the end of all formations, the forsaking of every substratum of rebirth, the fading away of craving, detachment, extinction, Nibbāna.

Yet there are beings whose eyes are only a little covered with dust: they will understand the truth. (MN 26)

I

The First Noble Truth

The Noble Truth of Suffering

What, now, is the noble truth of suffering?

Birth is suffering; decay is suffering; death is suffering; sorrow, lamentation, pain, grief, and despair are suffering; not to get what one desires is suffering; in short, the five groups of existence are suffering.

What now is birth? The birth of beings belonging to this or that order of beings, their being born, their conception and springing into existence, the manifestation of the groups of existence, the arising of sense activity: this is called birth.

And what is decay? The decay of beings belonging to this or that order of beings; their becoming aged, frail, gray, and wrinkled; the failing of their vital force, the wearing out of the senses: this is called decay.

And what is death? The departing and vanishing of beings out of this or that order of beings, their destruction, disappearance, death, the completion of their life-period, dissolution of the groups of existence, the discarding of the body: this is called death.

And what is sorrow? The sorrow arising through this or that loss or misfortune that one encounters, the worrying oneself, the state of being alarmed, inward sorrow, inward woe: this is called sorrow.

And what is lamentation? Whatsoever, through this or that loss or misfortune that befalls one, is wail and lament, wailing and lamenting, the state of woe and lamentation: this is called lamentation.

And what is pain? The bodily pain and unpleasantness, the painful and unpleasant feeling produced by bodily impression: this is called pain.

And what is grief? The mental pain and unpleasantness, the painful and unpleasant feeling produced by mental impression: this is called grief.

And what is despair? Distress and despair arising through this or that loss or misfortune that one encounters, distressfulness, and desperation: this is called despair.

And what is the "suffering of not getting what one desires"? To beings subject to birth there comes the desire: "Oh, that we were not subject to birth! Oh, that no new birth was before us!" Subject to decay, disease, death, sorrow, lamentation, pain, grief, and despair, the desire comes to them: "Oh, that we were not subject to these things! Oh, that these things were not before us!" But this cannot be got by mere desiring; and not to get what one desires is suffering. (DN 22)

THE FIVE GROUPS OF EXISTENCE
(*pañcupādānakkhandhā*)

And what, in brief, are the five groups of existence? They are corporeality, feeling, perception, (mental) formations, and consciousness. (DN 22)

All corporeal phenomena, whether past, present, or future, one's own or external, gross or subtle, lofty or low, far or near, all belong to the *group of corporeality*; all feelings belong to the *group of feeling*; all perceptions belong to the *group of perception*; all mental formations belong to the *group of mental formations*; all consciousness belongs to the *group of consciousness*. (MN 109)

These groups are a fivefold classification in which the Buddha has summed up all the physical and mental phenomena of existence, and in particular, those that appear to the ignorant man as his self or personality. Hence birth, decay, death, etc., are also included in these five groups which actually comprise the whole world.

The Group of Corporeality (*rūpa-khandha*)

What, now, is the *group of corporeality*? It is the four primary elements, and corporeality derived from them.

And what are the four primary elements? They are the solid element, the fluid element, the heating element, the vibrating (windy) element. (MN 28)

The four elements (*dhātu* or *mahā-bhūta*), popularly called earth, water, fire, and wind, are to be understood as the elementary qualities of matter. They are named in Pāli, *paṭhavī-dhātu, āpo-dhātu, tejo-dhātu, vāyo-dhātu*, and may be rendered as inertia, cohesion, radiation, and vibration. All four are present in every material object, though in varying degrees of strength. If, e.g., the earth element predominates, the material object is called "solid," etc.

The "corporeality derived from the four primary elements" (*upādāya rūpa* or *upādā rūpa*) consists, according to the Abhidhamma, of the following twenty-four material phenomena and qualities: eye, ear, nose, tongue, body, visible form, sound, odour, taste, masculinity, femininity, vitality, physical basis of mind (*hadaya-vatthu*; see B. Dict.), gesture, speech, space (cavities of ear, nose, etc.), decay, change, and nutriment.

Bodily impressions (*phoṭṭhabba*, the tactile) are not especially mentioned among these twenty-four, as they are identical with the solid, the heating, and the vibrating elements, which are cognizable through the sensations of pressure, cold, heat, pain, etc.

1. What, now, is the solid element (*paṭhavī-dhātu*)? The solid element may be one's own, or it may be external. And what is one's own solid element? Whatever in one's own person or body there exists of karmically acquired hardness, firmness, such as the hairs of head, hairs of body, nails, teeth, skin, flesh, sinews, bones, marrow, kidneys, heart, liver, diaphragm, spleen, lungs, stomach, bowels, mesentery, excrement, and so on: this is called one's own solid element. Now, whether it be one's own solid element, or whether it be the external solid element, they are both merely the solid element.

And one should understand, according to reality and true wisdom: "This does not belong to me; this am I not; this is not my self."

2. What, now, is the fluid element (*āpo-dhātu*)? The fluid element may be one's own, or it may be external. And what is one's own fluid element? Whatever in one's own person or body there exists of karmically acquired liquidity or fluidity, such as bile, phlegm, pus, blood, sweat, fat, tears, skin-grease, saliva, nasal mucus, oil of the joints, urine, and so on: this is called one's own fluid element. Now, whether it be one's own fluid element, or whether it be the external fluid element, they are both merely the fluid element.

And one should understand, according to reality and true wisdom: "This does not belong to me; this am I not; this is not my self."

3. What, now, is the heating element (*tejo-dhātu*)? The heating element may be one's own, or it may be external. And what is one's own heating element? Whatever in one's own person or body there exists of karmically acquired heat or hotness, such as that whereby one is heated, consumed,

scorched, that whereby what has been eaten, drunk, chewed, or tasted, is fully digested, and so on: this is called one's own heating element. Now, whether it be one's own heating element, or whether it be the external heating element, they are both merely the heating element.

And one should understand, according to reality and true wisdom: "This does not belong to me; this am I not; this is not my self."

4. What, now, is the vibrating (windy) element (*vāyo-dhātu*)? The vibrating element may be one's own, or it may be external. And what is one's own vibrating element? What in one's own person or body there exists of karmically acquired wind or windiness, such as the upward-going and downward-going winds, the winds of stomach and intestines, the wind permeating all the limbs, in-breathing and out-breathing, and so on: this is called one's own vibrating element. Now, whether it be one's own vibrating element or whether it be the external vibrating element, they are both merely the vibrating element.

And one should understand, according to reality and true wisdom: "This does not belong to me; this am I not; this is not my self."

Just as one calls "hut" the circumscribed space that comes to be by means of wood and rushes, reeds, and clay, even so we call "body" the circumscribed space that comes to be by means of bones and sinews, flesh and skin.

The Group of Feeling
(*vedanā-khandha*)

There are three kinds of feeling: pleasant, unpleasant, and neither pleasant nor unpleasant (indifferent). (SN 36:1)

The Group of perception
(*saññā-khandha*)

What, now, is perception? There are six classes of perception: perception of forms, sounds, odours, tastes, bodily impressions, and mental objects. (SN 22:56)

The Group of Mental formations
(*saṅkhāra-khandha*)

What, now, are mental formations? There are six classes of volition (*cetanā*): volition directed to forms (*rūpa-sañcetanā*), sounds, odours, tastes, bodily impressions, and mental objects. (SN 22:56)

The "group of mental formations" (*saṅkhāra-khandha*) is a collective term for numerous functions or aspects of mental activity which, in addition to feeling and perception, are present in a single moment of consciousness. In the Abhidhamma, fifty mental formations are distinguished, seven of which are constant factors of mind. The number and composition of the rest varies according to the character of the respective class of consciousness (see Table in B. Dict.).

In the Discourse on Right Understanding (MN 9) three main representatives of the group of mental formations are mentioned: volition (*cetanā*), sense impression (*phassa*), and attention (*manasikāra*). Of these again, it is volition which, being a principal "formative" factor, is particularly characteristic of the group of formations, and therefore serves to exemplify it in the passage given above.

For other applications of the term *saṅkhāra,* see B. Dict.

The Group of Consciousness
(*viññāṇa-khandha*)

What, now, is consciousness? There are six classes of consciousness: consciousness of forms, sounds, odours, tastes, bodily impressions, and mind-objects (lit.: eye-consciousness, ear-consciousness, etc.). (SN 22:56)

Dependent Origination of Consciousness

Now, though one's eye be intact, yet if the external forms do not fall within the field of vision, and no corresponding conjunction (of eye and forms) takes place, in that case there occurs no formation of the corresponding aspect of consciousness. Or, though one's eye be intact, and the external forms fall within the field of vision, yet if no corresponding conjunction takes place, in that case too there occurs no formation of the corresponding aspect of consciousness. If, however, one's eye is intact, and the external forms fall within the field of vision, and the corresponding conjunction takes place, in that case there arises the corresponding aspect of consciousness. (MN 28)

Hence I say: the arising of consciousness is dependent upon conditions; and without these conditions, no consciousness arises. And upon whatsoever conditions the arising of consciousness is dependent, after these it is called.

Consciousness, whose arising depends on the eye and forms, is called eye-consciousness (*cakkhu-viññāṇa*).

Consciousness, whose arising depends on the ear and sounds, is called ear-consciousness (*sota-viññāṇa*).

Consciousness, whose arising depends on the olfactory organ and odours, is called nose-consciousness (*ghāna-viññāṇa*).

Consciousness, whose arising depends on the tongue and tastes, is called tongue-consciousness (*jivhā-viññāṇa*).

Consciousness, whose arising depends on the body and bodily impressions, is called body-consciousness (*kāya-viññāṇa*).

Consciousness, whose arising depends on the mind and mind-objects, is called mind-consciousness (*mano-viññāṇa*).

(MN 28) Whatsoever there is of corporeality (*rūpa*) on that occasion, this belongs to the group of corporeality. Whatsoever there is of feeling (*vedanā*), this belongs to the group of feeling. Whatsoever there is of perception (*saññā*), this belongs to the group of perception. Whatsoever there are of mental formations (*saṅkhārā*), these belong to the group of mental formations. Whatsoever there is of consciousness (*viññāṇa*), this belongs to the group of consciousness. (MN 38)

Dependency of Consciousness on the Other Four Khandhas

And it is impossible for anyone to explain the passing out of one existence, and the entering into a new existence, or the growth, increase, and development of consciousness, independently of corporeality, feeling, perception, and mental formations. (SN 22:53)

The Three Characteristics of Existence (*tilakkhaṇa*)

All formations are transient (*anicca*); all formations are subject to suffering (*dukkha*); all things are not-self (*anattā*). (AN 3:134)

Corporeality is transient, feeling is transient, perception is transient, mental formations are transient, consciousness is transient. (SN 22:59)

And that which is transient, is subject to suffering; and of that which is transient and subject to suffering and change, one cannot rightly say: "This belongs to me; this am I; this is my self."

Therefore, whatever there is of corporeality, feeling, perception, mental formations, or consciousness, whether past, present, or future, one's own or external, gross or subtle, lofty or low, far or near, one should understand according to reality and true wisdom: "This does not belong to me; this am I not; this is not my self."

The Anattā Doctrine

Individual existence, as well as the whole world, is in reality nothing but a process of ever-changing phenomena which are all comprised in the five groups of existence. This process has gone on from time immemorial, before one's birth, and also after one's death it will continue for endless periods of time, as long, and as far, as there are conditions for it. As stated in the preceding texts, the five groups of existence—either taken separately or combined—in no way constitute a real ego-entity or subsisting personality, and equally no self, soul, or substance can be found outside of these groups as their "owner." In other words, the five groups of existence are "not-self" (*anattā*), nor do they belong to a self (*anattaniya*). In view of the impermanence and conditionality of all existence, the belief in any form of self must be regarded as an illusion.

Just as what we designate by the name "chariot" has no existence apart from axle, wheels, shaft, body, and so forth, or as the word "house" is merely a convenient designation for various materials put together after a certain fashion so as to enclose a portion of space, and there is no separate house-entity in existence, in exactly the same way that which we call a "being" or an "individual," or a "person," or by the name "I," is nothing but a changing combination of physical and mental phenomena, and has no real existence in itself.

This is, in brief, the *anattā* doctrine of the Buddha, the teaching that all existence is void (*suñña*) of a permanent self or substance. It is the fundamental Buddhist doctrine, not found in any other religious teaching or philosophical system. To grasp it fully, not only in an abstract and intellectual way, but by constant reference to actual experience, is an indispensable condition for the true understanding of the Buddha-Dhamma and for the realization of its goal. The *anattā* doctrine is the necessary outcome of the thorough analysis of actuality undertaken, e.g., in the doctrine of the five aggregates, of which only a bare indication can be given by means of the texts included here.

For a detailed survey of the *khandhas*, see B. Dict.

Suppose a man with good sight beheld the many bubbles on the Ganges as they drove along, and he watched them and carefully examined them; then after he had carefully examined them they would appear to him empty, unreal, and unsubstantial. In exactly the same way does the monk behold all the corporeal phenomena, feelings, perceptions, mental formations, and states of consciousness—whether they be of the past, or the present, or the future, far or near. And he watches them, and examines them carefully; and, after carefully examining them, they appear to him empty, void, and without a self. (SN 22:95)

Whoever delights in corporeality, or feeling, or perception, or mental formations, or consciousness, he delights in suffering; and whoever delights in suffering, will not be freed from suffering. Thus I say. (SN 22:29)

How can you find delight and mirth
Where there is burning without end?
In deepest darkness you are wrapped!
Why do you not seek for the light?

Look at this puppet here, well rigged,
A heap of many sores, piled up,
Diseased, and full of greediness,
Unstable, and impermanent!

Devoured by old age is this frame,
A prey to sickness, weak and frail;
To pieces breaks this putrid body,
All life must truly end in death. (Dhp 146–48)

The Three Warnings

Did you never see in the world a man or a woman, eighty, ninety, or a hundred years old, frail, crooked as a gable-roof, bent down, resting on crutches, with tottering steps, infirm, youth long since fled, with broken teeth, grey and scanty hair or none, wrinkled, with blotched limbs? And did the thought never come to you that you too are subject to decay, that you too cannot escape it?

Did you never see in the world a man or a woman who, being sick, afflicted, and grievously ill, wallowing in his own filth, was lifted up by some and put to bed by others? And did the thought never come to you that you too are subject to disease, that you too cannot escape it?

Did you never see in the world the corpse of a man or a woman, one or two or three days after death, swollen up, blue-black in colour, and full of corruption? And did the thought never come to you that you too are subject to death, that you too cannot escape it? (AN 3:35)

Saṃsāra

Inconceivable is the beginning of this saṃsāra; not to be discovered is any first beginning of beings, who, obstructed by ignorance and ensnared by craving, are hurrying and hastening through this round of rebirths. (SN 15:3)

Saṃsāra—the wheel of existence, lit. the "perpetual wandering"—is the name given in the Pāli scriptures to the sea of life ever restlessly heaving up and down, the symbol of this continuous process of ever again and again being born, growing old, suffering, and dying. More precisely put: *saṃsāra* is the unbroken sequence of the fivefold *khandha*-combinations, which, constantly changing from moment to moment, follow continually one upon the other through inconceivable periods of time. Of this saṃsāra, a single lifetime constitutes only a tiny fraction. Hence, to be able to comprehend the first noble truth, one must let one's gaze rest upon the saṃsāra, upon this frightful sequence of rebirths, and not merely upon one single lifetime, which, of course, may sometimes be not very painful.

The term "suffering" (*dukkha*) in the first noble truth therefore refers not merely to painful bodily and mental sensations due to unpleasant impressions, but comprises in addition everything productive of suffering or liable to it. The truth of suffering teaches that, owing to the universal law of impermanence, even high and sublime states of happiness are subject to change and destruction, and that all states of existence are therefore unsatisfactory, without exception carrying in themselves the seeds of suffering.

Which do you think is more: the flood of tears that, weeping and wailing, you have shed upon this long way—hurrying and hastening through this round of rebirths, united with the undesired, separated from the desired—this, or the waters of the four oceans? (SN 15:3)

Long have you suffered the death of father and mother, of sons, daughters, brothers, and sisters. And while you were thus suffering, you have indeed shed more tears upon this long way than there is water in the four oceans.

Which do you think is more: the streams of blood that, through your being beheaded, have flowed upon this long way—these, or the waters of the four oceans?

Long have you been caught as robbers or highway men or adulterers; and, through your being beheaded, truly more blood has flowed upon this long way than there is water in the four oceans.

But how is this possible?

Inconceivable is the beginning of this saṃsāra; not to be discovered is any first beginning of beings, who, obstructed by ignorance and ensnared by craving, are hurrying and hastening through this round of rebirths. (SN 15:13)

And thus have you long undergone suffering, undergone torment, undergone misfortune, and filled the graveyards full; truly, long enough to be dissatisfied with all forms of existence, long enough to turn away and free yourselves from them all. (SN 15:1)

II

The Second Noble Truth

The Noble Truth of the Origin of Suffering

What, now, is the noble truth of the origin of suffering? It is craving, which gives rise to fresh rebirth, and, bound up with pleasure and lust, now here, now there, finds ever-fresh delight. (SN 56:11)

The Threefold Craving

There is sensual craving (*kāma-taṇhā*), craving for (eternal) existence (*bhava-taṇhā*), craving for self-annihilation (*vibhava-taṇhā*). (DN 22)

Sensual craving (*kāma-taṇhā*) is the desire for the enjoyment of the five sense objects.

Craving for existence (*bhava-taṇhā*) is the desire for continued or eternal life, referring in particular to life in those higher worlds called fine-material and immaterial existences (*rūpa-*, and *arūpa-bhava*). It is closely connected with the so-called eternity-belief (*bhava-* or *sassata-diṭṭhi*), i.e., the belief in an absolute, eternal self persisting independently of our body.

Craving for self-annihilation (lit., "for non-existence," *vibhava-taṇhā*) is the outcome of the belief in annihilation (*vibhava-* or *uccheda-diṭṭhi*), i.e., the delusive materialistic notion of a more or less real self which is annihilated at death, and which does not stand in any causal relation with the time before death and the time after death.

The Origin of Craving

But where does this craving arise and take root? Wherever in the world there are delightful and pleasurable things, there this craving arises and takes root. Eye, ear, nose, tongue, body, and mind are delightful and pleasurable: there this craving arises and takes root. (DN 22)

Visual objects, sounds, smells , tastes, bodily impressions, and mind-objects are delightful and pleasurable: there this craving arises and takes root.

Consciousness, sense impression, feeling born of sense impression, perception, will, craving, thinking, and reflecting are delightful and pleasurable: there this craving arises and takes root.

This is called the noble truth of the origin of suffering.

Dependent Origination of all Phenomena

If, when perceiving a visual object, sound, odour, taste, bodily impression, or mental object, the object is pleasant, one is attracted; and if the object is unpleasant, one is repelled. (MN 38)

Thus, whatever kind of feeling (*vedanā*) one experiences—pleasant, unpleasant, or indifferent—if one approves of and cherishes the feeling, and clings to it, then while doing so, lust springs up; but lust for feelings means clinging (*upādāna*), and on clinging depends the (present) process of becoming; on the process of becoming (*bhava*; here *kamma-bhava*, karma-process) depends (future) birth (*jāti*); and dependent on birth are decay and death, sorrow, lamentation, pain, grief, and despair. Thus arises this whole mass of suffering.

The formula of dependent origination (*paṭicca-samuppāda*), of which only some of the twelve links have been mentioned in the preceding passage, may be regarded as a detailed explanation of the second noble truth.

Present Karma-Results

Truly, due to sensuous craving, conditioned through sensuous craving, impelled by sensuous craving, entirely moved by sensuous craving, kings fight with kings, princes with princes, priests with priests, citizens with citizens; the mother quarrels with the son, the son with the mother, the father with the son, the son with the father; brother quarrels with brother, brother with sister, sister with brother, friend with friend. Thus, given to dissension, quarrelling, and fighting, they fall upon one another with fists, sticks, or weapons. And thereby they suffer death or deadly pain.

And further, due to sensuous craving, conditioned through sensuous craving, impelled by sensuous craving, entirely moved by sensuous craving, people break into houses, rob, plunder, pillage whole houses, commit highway robbery, seduce the wives of others. Then the rulers have such people caught and inflict on them various forms of punishment. And thereby they incur death or deadly pain. Now, this is the misery of sensuous craving, the heaping up of suffering in this present life, due to sensuous craving, conditioned through sensuous craving, caused by sensuous craving, entirely dependent on sensuous craving.

Future Karma-Results

And further, people take the evil way in deeds, words, and thoughts; and by taking the evil way in deeds, words, and thoughts, at the dissolution of the body, after death, they fall into a downward state of existence, a state of suffering, into an unhappy destiny, the abyss of the hells. But this is the misery of sensuous craving, the heaping up of suffering in the future life, due to sensuous craving, conditioned through sensuous craving, caused by sensuous craving, entirely dependent on sensuous craving. (MN 13)

> Not in the air, nor ocean-midst,
> Nor hidden in the mountain clefts,
> Nowhere is found a place on earth,
> Where one is freed from evil deeds. (Dhp 127)

Karma as Volition

It is volition (*cetanā*) that I call karma (action). Having willed, one acts by body, speech, and mind.

There are actions (*kamma*) ripening in hells … ripening in the animal kingdom … ripening in the domain of ghosts … ripening amongst men … ripening in heavenly worlds.

The result of actions (*vipāka*) is of three kinds: ripening in the present life, in the next life, or in future lives. (AN 6:63)

Inheritance of Deeds

All beings are the owners of their deeds, the heirs of their deeds; their deeds, are the womb from which they sprang, with their deeds they are bound up, their deeds are their refuge. Whatever deeds they do—good or evil—of such they will be the heirs. (AN 10:206)

And wherever beings spring into existence, there their deeds will ripen; and wherever their deeds ripen, there they will earn the fruits of those deeds, be it in this life, or in the next life, or in any other future life. (AN 3:33)

There will come a time when the mighty ocean will dry up, vanish, and be no more. There will come a time when the mighty earth will be devoured by fire, perish, and be no more. But yet there will be no end to the suffering of beings, who, obstructed by ignorance and ensnared by craving, are hurrying and hastening through this round of rebirths. (SN 22:99)

Craving, however, is not the only cause of evil action, and thus of all the suffering and misery produced thereby in this and the next life; but wherever there is craving, there, dependent on craving, may arise envy, anger, hatred, and many other evil states productive of suffering and misery. And all these selfish, life-affirming impulses and actions, together with the various kinds of misery produced thereby here or hereafter, and even all the five groups of phenomena constituting life—everything is ultimately rooted in blindness and ignorance (*avijjā*).

Karma

The second noble truth serves also to explain the causes of the seeming injustices in nature, by teaching that nothing in the world can come into existence without reason or cause, and that not only our latent tendencies, but our whole destiny, all weal and woe, result from causes which we have to seek partly in this life, partly in former states of existence. These causes are the life-affirming activities (*kamma*, Skt: *karma*) produced by body, speech, and mind. Hence it is this threefold action that determines the character and destiny of all beings.

Exactly defined, karma denotes those good and evil volitions (*kusala-* and *akusala-cetanā*), causing rebirth and shaping the destinies of beings. Thus existence—or better, the process of becoming (*bhava*)—consists of an active and conditioning karma process (*kamma-bhava*), and its result, the rebirth process (*upapatti-bhava*).

Here, too, when considering karma, one must not lose sight of the impersonal nature (*anattatā*) of existence. In the case of a storm-swept sea, it is not an identical wave that hastens over the surface of the ocean, but it is the rising and falling of quite different masses of water. In the same way it should be understood that there are no real ego-entities hastening through the ocean of rebirth, but merely life-waves, which, according to their nature and activities (good or evil), manifest themselves here as humans, there as animals, and elsewhere as invisible beings.

Once more the fact may be emphasized here that, correctly speaking, the term "karma" signifies only the aforementioned kinds of action themselves, and does not mean or include their results.

For further details about karma, see Fund. and B. Dict.

III

The Third Noble Truth

The Noble Truth of the Extinction of Suffering

What, now, is the noble truth of the extinction of suffering? It is the complete fading away and extinction of this craving, its forsaking and abandonment, liberation and detachment from it. (SN 56:11)

But where may this craving vanish, where may it be extinguished? Wherever in the world there are delightful and pleasurable things, there this craving may vanish, there it may be extinguished. (DN 22)

Be it in the past, present, or future, whatever monks or priests regard the delightful and pleasurable things in the world as impermanent (*anicca*), miserable (*dukkha*), and without a self (*anattā*), as diseases and cankers, it is they who overcome craving. (SN 12:66)

Dependent Extinction of all Phenomena

And through the total fading away and extinction of craving (*taṇhā*), clinging (*upādāna*) is extinguished; through the extinction of clinging, the process of becoming (*bhava*) is extinguished; through the extinction of the (karmic) process of becoming, rebirth (*jāti*) is extinguished; and through the extinction of rebirth, decay and death, sorrow, lamentation, pain, grief, and despair are extinguished. Thus comes about the extinction of this whole mass of suffering. (SN 12:43)

Hence the annihilation, cessation, and overcoming of corporeality, feeling, perception, mental formations, and consciousness—this is the extinction of suffering, the end of disease, the overcoming of old age and death. (SN 22:30)

The undulatory motion which we call a wave—and which in the ignorant spectator creates the illusion of one and the same mass of water moving over the surface of the lake—is produced and fed by the wind, and maintained by the stored-up energies. Now, after the wind has ceased, and if no fresh wind again whips up the water of the lake, the stored-up energies will gradually be consumed, and thus the whole undulatory motion will come to an end. Similarly, if fire does not get new fuel, it will, after consuming all the old fuel, become extinct.

Just in the same way this five-khandha process, which in the ignorant worldling creates the illusion of a self, is produced and fed by the life-affirming craving (*taṇhā*), and maintained for some time by means of the stored-up life energies. Now, after the fuel (*upādāna*), i.e., the craving and clinging to life, has ceased, and if no new craving impels again this five-khandha process, life will continue as long as there are still life-energies stored up, but at their destruction at death, the five-khandha process will reach final extinction.

Thus, Nibbāna or "extinction" (Skt.: *nirvāna*; from *nir* + *vā*, to cease blowing, become extinct) may be considered under two aspects, namely as:

1. "Extinction of impurities" (*kilesa-parinibbāna*), reached at the attainment of arahantship or holiness, which generally takes place during life; in the Suttas it is called *sa-upādisesa-nibbāna*, i.e., "Nibbāna with the groups of existence still remaining."

2. "Extinction of the five-khandha process" (*khandha-parinibbāna*), which takes place at the death of the arahant, called in the Suttas *an-upādisesa-nibbāna*, i.e., "Nibbāna without the groups remaining."

Nibbāna

This, truly, is peace, this is the highest, namely, the end of all karma formations, the forsaking of every substratum of rebirth, the fading away of craving, detachment, extinction, Nibbāna. (AN 3:32)

Enraptured with lust, enraged with hatred, blinded by delusion, overwhelmed, with mind ensnared, a man aims at his own ruin, at the ruin of others, at the ruin of both, and he experiences mental pain and grief. But if lust, hatred, and delusion are given up, a man aims neither at his own ruin, nor at the ruin of others, nor at the ruin of both, and he experiences no mental pain and grief. Thus is Nibbāna immediate, visible in this life, inviting, attractive, and comprehensible to the wise. (AN 3:55)

The extinction of greed, the extinction of hate, the extinction of delusion: this, indeed, is called Nibbāna. (SN 38:1)

The Arahant or Holy One

And for a disciple thus freed, in whose heart dwells peace, there is nothing to be added to what has been done, and nothing more remains for him to do. Just as a rock of one solid mass remains unshaken by the wind, even so neither forms, nor sounds, nor odours, nor tastes, nor contacts of any kind, neither the desired nor the undesired, can cause such a one to waver. Steadfast is his mind, gained is deliverance. (AN 6:55)

And he who has considered all the contrasts on this
earth,
And is no more disturbed by anything in the world,
The Peaceful One, freed from rage, sorrow, and longing,
Has passed beyond birth and decay. (Sn 1048)

The Immutable

Truly, there is a realm where there is neither the solid, nor the fluid, nor heat, nor motion, neither this world nor any other world, neither sun nor moon. This I call neither arising nor passing away, neither standing still nor being born nor dying. There is neither foothold nor development nor any basis. This is the end of suffering. (Ud 8:1)

There is an Unborn, Unoriginated, Uncreated, Unformed. If there were not this Unborn, Unoriginated, Uncreated, Unformed, escape from the world of the born, the originated, the created, the formed would not be possible. But since there is an Unborn, Unoriginated, Uncreated, Unformed, therefore escape is possible from the world of the born, the originated, the created, the formed. (Ud 8:3)

IV

The Fourth Noble Truth

The Noble Truth of the Path that leads to the Extinction of Suffering

To give oneself up to indulgence in sensual pleasure, the base, common, vulgar, unholy, unprofitable; or to give oneself up to self-mortification, the painful, unholy, unprofitable: both these two extremes, the Perfect One has avoided, and has found out the Middle Path, which makes one both see and know, which leads to peace, to discernment, to enlightenment, to Nibbāna. (SN 56:11)

THE NOBLE EIGHTFOLD PATH
(*ariya-aṭṭhaṅgikamagga*)

It is the Noble Eightfold Path, the way that leads to the extinction of suffering, namely:

1.	Right understanding *Sammā-diṭṭhi*	III. Wisdom *(paññā)*
2.	Right thought *Sammā-saṅkappa*	
3.	Right speech *Sammā-vācā*	I. Morality *(sīla)*
4.	Right action *Sammā-kammanta*	
5.	Right livelihood *Sammā-ājiva*	

6.	Right effort *Sammā-vāyāma*	II. Concentration (*samādhi*)
7.	Right mindfulness *Sammā-sati*	
8.	Right concentration *Sammā-samādhi*	

This is the Middle Path which the Perfect One has found out, which makes one both see and know, which leads to peace, to discernment, to enlightenment, to Nibbāna.

The figurative expression "path" or "way" has been sometimes misunderstood as implying that the single factors of the path have to be taken up for practice one after the other, in the order given. In that case, right understanding, i.e., the full penetration of truth, would have to be realized first, before one could think of developing right thought or of practicing right speech, etc. But in reality the three factors (3–5) forming the section "morality" (*sīla*) have to be perfected first; after that one has to give attention to the systematic training of mind by practising the three factors (6–8) forming the section "concentration" (*samādhi*); only after that preparation will one's character and mind be capable of reaching perfection in the first two factors (1–2) forming the section of "wisdom" (*paññā*).

An initial minimum of right understanding, however, is required at the very start, because some grasp of the facts of suffering, etc., is necessary to provide convincing reasons and an incentive for diligent practice of the path. A measure of right understanding is also required for helping the other path factors to fulfil intelligently and efficiently their individual functions in the common task of liberation. For that reason, and to emphasize the importance of that factor, right understanding has been given the first place in the Noble Eightfold Path.

This initial understanding of the Dhamma, however, has to be gradually developed, with the help of the other path factors, until it reaches finally that highest clarity of insight (*vipassanā*) that is the immediate condition for entering the four stages of holiness (see pp. 39 f.) and for attaining *Nibbāna*.

Right understanding is therefore the beginning as well as the culmination of the Noble Eightfold Path.

Free from pain and torture is this path, free from groaning and suffering: it is the perfect path. (MN 139)

> Truly, like this path there is no
> other path to the purity of insight.
> If you follow this path,
> you will put an end to suffering. (Dhp 274–75)

> But each one has to struggle for himself,
> The Perfect Ones have only pointed out the way.
> (Dhp 276)

Give ear, then, for the Deathless is found. I reveal, I set forth the truth. As I reveal it to you, so act! And that supreme goal of the holy life, for the sake of which sons of good families rightly go forth from home to the homeless state: this you will, in no long time, in this very life, make known to yourselves, realize, and make your own. (MN 26)

First Factor

Right Understanding
(*sammā-diṭṭhi*)

What now is right understanding?

Understanding the Four Noble Truths

(1) To understand suffering; (2) to understand the origin of suffering; (3) to understand the extinction of suffering; (4) to understand the path that leads to the extinction of suffering: this is called right understanding. (DN 22)

Understanding the Wholesome and Unwholesome

Again, when the noble disciple understands what is karmically wholesome, and the root of wholesome karma, what is karmically unwholesome, and the root of unwholesome karma, then he has right understanding.

What, now, is karmically unwholesome (*akusala*)?

1.	Destruction of living beings	Bodily action (*kāya-kamma*)
2.	Stealing	
3.	Unlawful sexual intercourse	
4.	Lying	Verbal action (*vacī-kamma*)
5.	Tale-bearing	
6.	Harsh speech	
7.	Frivolous talk	

8. Covetousness 9. Ill-will 10. Wrong views	}	Mental action (*mano-kamma*)

These things are karmically unwholesome.

> These ten are called unwholesome courses of action (*akusala-kammapatha*).

And what are the roots of unwholesome karma? Greed (*lobha*) is a root of unwholesome karma; hatred (*dosa*) is a root of unwholesome karma; delusion (*moha*) is a root of unwholesome karma.

Therefore, I say, these unwholesome actions are of three kinds: either due to greed, or due to hatred, or due to delusion.

> Every volitional act of body, speech, or mind, rooted in greed, hatred, or delusion, is regarded as karmically unwholesome or unskilful, as it produces evil and painful results in this life or in some future existence. The will or volition is really what counts as action (*kamma*). It may manifest outwardly itself as action of body or speech; if it does not manifest itself outwardly, it is counted as mental action.
>
> The state of greed (*lobha*), as also hatred (*dosa*), is always accompanied by ignorance (or delusion; *moha*), this latter being the primary root of all evil. Greed and hatred, however, cannot co-exist in one and the same moment of consciousness.

What, now, is karmically wholesome (*kusala*)?

1. To abstain from killing 2. To abstain from stealing 3. To abstain from unlawful sexual intercourse	}	Bodily action (*kāya-kamma*)

4.	To abstain from lying	Verbal action (*vacī-kamma*)
5.	To abstain from tale-bearing	
6.	To abstain from harsh speech	
7.	To abstain from frivolous talk	
8.	Absence of covetousness	Mental action (*mano-kamma*)
9.	Absence of ill-will	
10.	Right understanding	

These things are karmically wholesome.

These ten are called "wholesome courses of action" (*kusala-kammapatha*).

And what are the roots of wholesome karma? Absence of greed (*alobha* = unselfishness) is a root of wholesome karma; absence of hatred (*adosa* = kindness) is a root of wholesome karma; absence of delusion (*amoha* = wisdom) is a root of wholesome karma. (MN 9)

Understanding the Three Characteristics (*tilakkhaṇa*)

Again, when one understands that corporeality, feeling, perception, mental formations, and consciousness are transient (subject to suffering, and not self), also in that case one possesses right understanding. (SN 22:51)

Unprofitable Questions

Should anyone say that he does not wish to lead the holy life under the Blessed One, unless the Blessed One first tells him whether the world is eternal or temporal; finite or infinite; whether the life-principle is identical with the body or something different; whether the Perfect One continues after death, etc.—such a one would die before the Perfect One could tell him all this.

It is as if a man were pierced by a poisoned arrow, and his friends, companions, and relations should send for a surgeon; but that man should say: "I will not have this arrow pulled out until I know who the man is that has wounded me; whether he is a noble man, a priest, a tradesman, or a servant; or what his name is, and to what family he belongs; or whether he is tall, or short, or of medium height." Truly, such a man would die before he could adequately learn all this. (MN 63)

> Therefore, the man who seeks his own welfare,
> should pull out this arrow—
> this arrow of lamentation,
> of pain and sorrow. (Sn 592)

For, whether the theory exists, or whether it does not exist, that the world is eternal or temporal, or finite or infinite—yet certainly there exist birth, decay, and death, there exist sorrow, lamentation, pain, grief, and despair, the extinction of which, in this present life, I make known to you. (MN 63)

Five Fetters
(*saṃyojana*)

Suppose, for instance, that there is an unlearned worldling, void of regard for holy men, ignorant of the teaching of holy men, untrained in the noble doctrine. And his heart is possessed and overcome by self-illusion, by scepticism, by attachment to mere rule and ritual, by sensual lust, and by ill-will; and he does not in reality know how to free himself from these things. (MN 64)

Self-illusion (*sakkāya-diṭṭhi*) may reveal itself as:

1. "Eternalism" (*bhava-* or *sassata-diṭṭhi*, lit. "eternity-belief"), i.e., the belief that one's ego, self, or soul exists independently of the material body, and continues even after the dissolution of the latter.

2. "Annihilationism" (*vibhava-* or *uccheda-diṭṭhi*, lit. "annihilation-belief"), i.e., the materialistic belief that this present life constitutes the self and hence that the self is annihilated at the death of the material body.

For the ten fetters (*saṃyojana*), see p. 39.

Unwise Considerations

Not knowing what is worthy of consideration and what is unworthy of consideration, he considers the unworthy, and not the worthy.

And unwisely he considers thus: "Have I been in the past? Or, have I not been in the past? What have I been in the past? How have I been in the past? From what state into what state did I change in the past? Shall I be in the future? Or, shall I not be in the future? What shall I be in the future? How shall I be in the future? From what state into what state shall I change in the future?" And the present also fills him with doubt: "Am I? Or am I not? What am I? How am I? This being, whence has it come? Where will it go?"

The Six Views About the Self

And with such unwise considerations, he adopts one or other of six views, and it becomes his conviction and firm belief: "I have a self"; or: "I have no self"; or: "With the self I perceive the self"; or: "With that which is no self, I perceive the self"; or: "With the self I perceive that which is no self." Or he adopts the following view: "This my self, which can think and feel, and which, now here, now there, experiences the fruit of good and evil deeds—this my self is permanent, stable, eternal, not subject to change, and will thus eternally remain the same." (MN 2)

If there really existed the self, there would also exist something which belonged to the self. As, however, in truth and reality neither the self nor anything belonging to the self can be found, is it not therefore really an utter fools' doctrine to say: "This is the world, this is the self; after death I shall be permanent, persisting, and eternal"? (MN 22)

These are called mere views, a thicket of views, a puppet-show of views, a toil of views, a snare of views; and ensnared in the fetter of views, the ignorant worldling will not be freed from rebirth, from decay, from death, from sorrow, lamentation, pain, grief, and despair; he will not be freed, I say, from suffering.

Wise Considerations

The learned and noble disciple, however, who has regard for holy men, who knows the teaching of holy men, who is well trained in the noble doctrine, understands what is worthy of consideration and what is unworthy. And knowing this, he considers the worthy and not the unworthy. He wisely considers what suffering is; he wisely considers what the origin of suffering is; he wisely considers what the extinction of suffering is; he wisely considers what the path is that leads to the extinction of suffering. (MN 2)

The Sotāpanna or Stream-Enterer

And by thus considering, three fetters vanish, namely: self-illusion, scepticism, and attachment to mere rule and ritual.

But those disciples, in whom these three fetters have vanished, they all have entered the stream. (MN 22)

Better than any earthly power,
Better than all the joys of heaven,
Better than rule over all the world
Is the entrance to the stream. (Dhp 178)

The Ten Fetters
(*saṃyojana*)

There are ten "fetters" (*saṃyojana*) by which beings are bound to the wheel of existence. They are: (1) self-illusion (*sakkāya-diṭṭhi*), (2) scepticism (*vicikicchā*), (3) attachment to mere rule and ritual (*sīlabbata-parāmāsa*), (4) sensual lust (*kāmarāga*), (5) ill-will (*vyāpāda*), (6) craving for fine-material existence (*rūpa-rāga*), (7) craving for immaterial existence (*arūpa-rāga*), (8) conceit (*māna*), (9) restlessness (*uddhacca*), (10) ignorance (*avijjā*).

The Noble Ones
(*ariya-puggala*)

One who is freed from the first three fetters is called a *sotāpanna,* stream-enterer, i.e., one who has entered the stream leading to Nibbāna. He has unshakable faith in the Buddha, Dhamma, and Sangha, and is incapable of breaking the five moral precepts. He will be reborn seven times at the utmost, and not in a state lower than the human world.

One who has overcome the fourth and fifth fetters in their grosser form is called a *sakadāgāmi*, once-returner. He will be reborn only once more in the sensuous sphere (*kāma-loka*), and thereafter attain Nibbāna.

An *anāgāmi*, "non-returner," is wholly freed from the first five fetters which bind one to rebirth in the sensuous sphere; after death, while living in the fine-material sphere (*rūpa-loka*), he will reach the goal.

An *arahant*, i.e., the perfectly holy one, is freed from all the ten fetters.

Each of the aforementioned four stages of holiness consists of the "path" (*magga*) and the "fruition" (*phala*), e.g., "path of stream-entry" (*sotāpatti-magga*) and "fruition of stream-entry" (*sotāpatti-phala*). Accordingly there are eight types, or four pairs, of "noble individuals" (*ariya-puggala*).

The "path" consists of the single moment of entering the respective attainment. By "fruition" is meant those moments of consciousness which follow immediately thereafter as the result of the path, and which under certain circumstances may be repeated innumerable times during one's lifetime.

For further details, see B. Dict.: *ariya-puggala*, *sotāpanna*, etc.

Therefore, I say, right understanding is of two kinds:

Mundane and Supramundane Understanding

1. The view that alms and offerings are not useless; that there is fruit and result, both of good and bad actions; that there are such things as this life and the next life; that father and mother, as also spontaneously born beings (in the heavenly worlds), are not mere words; that there are in the world monks and priests, who are spotless and perfect, who can explain this life and the next life, which they themselves have understood: this is called the "mundane right understanding" (*lokiya-sammā-diṭṭhi*), which yields worldly fruits and brings good results.

2. But whatsoever there is of wisdom, of penetration, of right understanding conjoined with the path (of the *sotāpanna*,

sakadāgāmi, anāgāmi, or *arahant*)—the mind being turned away from the world and conjoined with the path, the holy path being pursued: this is called the "supramundane right understanding" (*lokuttara-sammā-diṭṭhi*), which is not of the world, but is supramundane and conjoined with the path.

> Thus, there are two kinds of eightfold path: (1) the mundane (*lokiya*), practised by the worldling (*puthujjana*), i.e., by all those who have not yet reached the first stage of holiness; *and* (2) the supramundane (*lokuttara*) practised by the noble ones (*ariya-puggala*).

Conjoined with Other Steps

Now, in understanding wrong understanding as wrong and right understanding as right, one practises *right understanding* (1st factor); and in making efforts to overcome wrong understanding, and to arouse right understanding, one practises *right effort* (6th factor); and in overcoming wrong understanding with attentive mind, and dwelling with attentive mind in the possession of right understanding, one practises *right mindfulness* (7th factor). Hence, there are three things that accompany and follow upon right understanding, namely: right understanding, right effort, and right mindfulness. (MN 117)

Free from All Theories

Now, if anyone should put the question, whether I admit any theory at all, he should be answered thus:

The Perfect One is free from any theory, for the Perfect One has understood what corporeality is, and how it arises and passes away. He has understood what feeling is, and how it arises and passes away. He has understood what perception is, and how it arises and passes away. He has understood what the mental formations are, and how they arise and pass away. He has understood what consciousness is, and how it arises and passes away. Therefore, I say, the Perfect One has won complete deliverance through the extinction, fading away, disappearance, rejection, and getting rid of all opinions and conjectures, of all inclination to the vain-glory of "I" and "mine." (MN 72)

THE THREE CHARACTERISTICS

Whether Perfect Ones (Buddhas) appear in the world, or whether Perfect Ones do not appear in the world, it still remains a firm condition, an immutable fact and fixed law: that all formations are impermanent (*anicca*); that all formations are subject to suffering (*dukkha*); that everything is not self (*anattā*). (AN 3:134)

In Pāli: *sabbe saṅkhārā aniccā, sabbe saṅkhārā dukkhā, sabbe dhammā anattā.*

The word "*saṅkhārā*" (formations) comprises here all things that are conditioned or "formed" (*saṅkhata-dhamma*), i.e., all possible physical and mental constituents of existence. The word "*dhamma*," however, has a still wider application and is all-embracing, as it comprises also the so-called Unconditioned ('unformed", *asaṅkhata*), i.e., Nibbāna.

For this reason, it would be wrong to say that all *dhammas* are impermanent and subject to change, for the Nibbāna-dhamma is permanent and free from change. And for the same reason, it is correct to say that not only all the *saṅkhāras* (= *saṅkhata-dhamma*), but all the *dhammas* (including the *asaṅkhata-dhamma*) lack a self (*anattā*).

A corporeal phenomenon, a feeling, a perception, a mental formation, a consciousness, which is permanent and persistent, eternal and not subject to change, such a thing the wise men in this world do not recognize; and I too say that there is no such thing. (SN 22:94)

And it is impossible that a being possessed of right understanding should regard anything as the self. (AN 1:15)

Views and Discussions about the Self

Now, if someone should say that feeling is his self, he should be answered thus: "There are three kinds of feeling: pleasurable, painful, and indifferent feeling. Which of these three feelings do you consider as your self?" Because, at the moment of experiencing one of these feelings, one does not experience the other two. These three kinds of feeling are impermanent, of dependent origin, are subject to decay and dissolution, to fading away and extinction. Whoever, in experiencing one of these feelings, thinks that this is his self must, after the extinction of that feeling, admit that his self has become dissolved. And thus he will consider his self already in this present life as impermanent, mixed up with pleasure and pain, subject to arising and passing away.

If anyone should say that feeling is not his self, and that his self is inaccessible to feeling, he should be asked thus: "Now, where there is no feeling, is it then possible to say: "This am I?'"

Or, another might say: "Feeling, indeed, is not my self, but it is also untrue that my self is inaccessible to feeling; for it is my self that feels, my self that has the faculty of feeling." Such a one should be answered thus: "Suppose that feeling should become altogether totally extinguished; now, if after the extinction of feeling, no feeling whatever exists there, is it then possible to say: 'This am I'?" (DN 15)

To assert that the mind, or the mind-objects, or mind-consciousness constitute the self—such an assertion is unfounded. For an arising and passing away is seen there; and seeing the arising and passing away of these things, one would come to the conclusion that one's self arises and passes away. (MN 148)

It would be better for the unlearned worldling to regard his body, built up of the four elements, as his self, rather than his mind. For it is evident that the body may last for a year, or two years, or three, four, five, or ten years, or even for a hundred years and more; but that which is called thought, or mind, or consciousness, arises continuously during day and night as one thing, and passes away as another thing. (SN 12:61)

Therefore, whatever there is of corporeality, feeling, perception, mental formations, or consciousness, whether past, present, or future, one's own or external, gross or subtle, lofty or low, far or near: of this one should understand according to reality and true wisdom: "This does not belong to me; this am I not; this is not my self." (SN 22:59)

> To show the impersonality and utter emptiness of existence, Vism XVI.90 quotes the following verse:
>
> *Mere suffering exists, no sufferer is found;*
> *The deed is, but no doer of the deed is there.*
> *Nirvāna is, but not the man that enters it.*
> *The path is, but no traveller on it is seen.*

Past, Present, and Future

Now, if anyone should ask: "Have you been in the past, and is it untrue that you have not been? Will you be in the future, and is it untrue that you will not be? Are you now, and is it untrue that you are not?"—you may reply that you have been in the past, and that it is untrue that you have not been; that you will be in the future, and that it is untrue that you will not be; that you are, and that it is untrue that you are not.

In the past only that past existence was real, but unreal the future and present existence. In the future only the future existence will be real, but unreal the past and the present existence. Now only the present existence is real, but unreal the past and future existence. (DN 9)

One who perceives dependent origination (*paṭicca-samuppāda*), perceives the truth; and one who percieves the truth, perceives dependent origination. (MN 28)

For just as from the cow comes milk, from milk curd, from curd butter, from butter ghee, from ghee the skim of ghee; and when it is milk, it is not counted as curd, or butter, or ghee, or skim of ghee, but only as milk; and when it is curd, it is only counted as curd; just so was my past existence at that time real, but unreal the future and present existence; and my future existence will be at that time real, but unreal the past and present existence; and my present existence is now real, but unreal the past and future existence. All these are merely popular designations and expressions, mere conventional terms of speaking, mere popular notions. The Perfect One indeed makes use of these, without however clinging to them. (DN 9)

Thus, one who does not understand corporeality, feeling, perception, mental formations, and consciousness according to reality (i.e., as void of a self) nor understands their arising, their extinction, and the way to their extinction, he is liable to believe either that the Perfect One continues after death, or that he does not continue after death, and so forth. (SN 44:4)

The Two Extremes and the Middle Doctrine

Truly, if one holds the view that the vital principle (*jīva*; "soul") is identical with this body, in that case a holy life is not possible; and if one holds the view that the vital principle is something quite different from the body, in that case also a holy life is not possible. Both these two extremes the Perfect One has avoided, and he has shown the Middle Doctrine of dependent origination. (SN 12:25)

Dependent Origination
(paṭicca-samuppāda)

On ignorance (*avijjā*) depend the karma-formations (*saṅkhārā*). On the karma-formations depends consciousness (*viññāṇa*; starting with rebirth-consciousness in the womb of the mother). On consciousness depends the mental and physical existence (*nāma-rūpa*). On the mental and physical existence depend the six sense organs (*saḷāyatana*). On the six sense organs depends sensorial impression (*phassa*). On sensorial impression depends feeling (*vedanā*). On feeling depends craving (*taṇhā*). On craving depends clinging (*upādāna*). On clinging depends the process of becoming (*bhava*). On the process of becoming (here: *kamma-bhava*, or karma-process) depends rebirth (*jāti*). On rebirth depend decay and death (*jarā-maraṇa*), sorrow, lamentation, pain, grief, and despair. Thus arises this whole mass of suffering. This is called the noble truth of the origin of suffering. (SN 12:1)

No god, no Brahmā, can be called
The maker of this wheel of life;
Empty phenomena roll on,
Dependent on conditions all.

Quoted in Vism XIX.20

A disciple, however, in whom ignorance has disappeared and wisdom arisen, such a disciple heaps up neither meritorious, nor demeritorious, nor imperturbable karma-formations. (SN 12:51)

The term "*saṅkhārā*" has been rendered here by "karma-formations" because, in the context of dependent origination, it refers to karmically wholesome and unwholesome volition (*cetanā*), or volitional activity, in short, karma.

Its threefold division, given in the preceding passage, comprises karmic activity in all spheres of existence or planes of consciousness. The "meritorious karma-formations" extend also to the fine-material sphere (*rūpāvacara*), while the "imperturbable karma-formations" (*āneñjābhi-saṅkhārā*) refer only to the immaterial sphere (*arūpāvacara*).

Thus, through the entire fading away and extinction of this ignorance, the karma-formations are extinguished. Through the extinction of karma-formations, consciousness (rebirth) is extinguished. Through the extinction of consciousness, the mental and physical existence is extinguished. Through the extinction of the mental and physical existence, the six sense organs are extinguished. Through the extinction of the six sense organs, sensorial impression is extinguished. Through the extinction of sensorial impression, feeling is extinguished. Through the extinction of feeling, craving is extinguished. Through the extinction of craving, clinging is extinguished. Through the extinction of clinging, the process of becoming is extinguished. Though the extinction of the process of becoming, rebirth is extinguished. Through the extinction of rebirth, decay and death, sorrow, lamentation, pain, grief, and despair are extinguished. Thus takes place the extinction of this whole mass of suffering. This is called the noble truth of the extinction of suffering.

(SN 12:1)

Rebirth-Producing Karma

Truly, because beings, obstructed by ignorance (*avijjā*) and ensnared by craving (*taṇhā*), seek ever fresh delight, now here, now there, therefore fresh rebirth continually comes to be. (MN 43)

And the action (*kamma*) that is done out of greed, hatred, and delusion (*lobha, dosa, moha*), that springs from them, has its source and origin in them: this action ripens wherever one is reborn, and wherever this action ripens there one experiences the fruits of this action, be it in this life, or in the next life, or in some future life. (AN 3:33)

Cessation of karma

However, through the fading away of ignorance, through the arising of wisdom, through the extinction of craving, no future rebirth takes place again. (MN 43)

For the actions which are not done out of greed, hatred, and delusion, which have not sprung from them, which have not their source and origin in them: such actions, through the absence of greed, hatred, and delusion, are abandoned, rooted out, like a palm-tree torn out of the soil, destroyed, and not able to spring up again. (AN 3:33)

In this respect one may rightly say of me: that I teach annihilation, that I propound my doctrine for the purpose of annihilation, and that I herein train my disciples; for certainly I do teach annihilation—the annihilation, namely, of greed, hatred, and delusion, as well as of the manifold evil and unwholesome things. (AN 8:12)

Paṭicca-samuppāda, lit. dependent origination, is the doctrine of the conditionality of all physical and mental phenomena. This doctrine, together with that of non-self (*anattā*), forms the indispensable condition for the real understanding and realization of the Buddha's teaching. It shows that the various physical and mental life-processes, conventionally called personality, man, animal, etc., are not a mere play of blind chance, but the outcome of causes and conditions. Above all, *paṭicca-samuppāda* explains how the arising of rebirth and suffering is dependent upon conditions; and in its second part, it shows how, through the removal of these conditions, all suffering must disappear. Hence, *paṭicca-samuppāda* serves to elucidate the second and the third noble truths, by explaining them from their very foundations upwards, and giving them a fixed philosophical form.

Accordingly it is said in the Paṭisambhidāmagga:

Five causes were there in the past,
Five fruits we find in the present life.
Five causes do we now produce,
Five fruits we reap in the future life.

(Quoted in Vism XVII.291)

For a full explanation, see Fund. III and B. Dict.

This diagram shows at a glance how the twelve links of the formula extend over three consecutive existences, past, present, and future.

3 periods of time	*12 factors or nidānas*	*4 groups of 5 modes each*	*20 modes*
Past	*1. Ignorance* *2. Karma-formations*	*Karma-process (kamma-bhava)* *5 karmic causes 1, 2, 8, 9, 10*	*Five causes in the past,*
Present	*3. Consciousness* *4. Mind & body* *5. The six bases* *6. Impression* *7. Feeling*	*Rebirth Process (uppatti-bhava)* *5 Karma results: 3–7*	*and now a fivefold fruit*
	8. Craving *9. Clinging* *10. Process of becoming*	*Karma process (kamma-bhava)* *5 karmic causes: 1, 2, 8, 9, 10*	*Five causes now,*
Future	*11. Rebirth* *12. Decay & death*	*Rebirth-process (uppatti-bhava)*	*and yet to come a fivefold fruit.*

The links 1–2, together with 8–10, represent the karma-process, containing the five karmic causes of rebirth.

The links 3–7, together with 11–12, represent the rebirth-process, containing the five karma-results.

Second Factor

Right Thought
(*sammā-saṅkappa*)

What now is right thought?

1. Thought free from lust (*nekkhamma-saṅkappa*).
2. Thought free from ill-will (*avyāpāda-saṅkappa*).
3. Thought free from cruelty (*avihiṃsā-saṅkappa*).

This is called right thought. (DN 22)

Mundane and Supramundane Right Thought

Now right thought, I tell you, is of two kinds:

1. Thought free from lust, from ill-will, and from cruelty—this is called mundane right thought (*lokiya sammā-saṅkappa*), which yields worldly fruits and brings good results.

2. But, whatsoever there is of thinking, considering, reasoning, thought, ratiocination, application—the mind being holy, being turned away from the world, and conjoined with the path, the holy path being pursued—these "verbal operations" of the mind (*vacī-saṅkhārā*) are called supramundane right thought (*lokuttara sammā-saṅkappa*), which is not of the world, but is supramundane and conjoined with the path.

Conjoined with Other Factors

Now, in understanding wrong thought as wrong, and right thought as right, one practises *right understanding* (1st factor); and in making efforts to overcome wrong thought and to arouse right thought, one practises *right effort* (6th factor); and in overcoming wrong thought with attentive mind, and dwelling with attentive mind in possession of right thought, one practises *right mindfulness* (7th factor). Hence there are three things that accompany and follow upon right thought, namely: right understanding, right effort, and right mindfulness. (MN 117)

Third Factor

Right Speech
(*sammā-vācā*)

What now is right speech? Abstaining from lying, abstaining from tale-bearing, abstaining from harsh language, abstaining from vain talk. (DN 22)

1. Abstaining from Lying

Herein someone avoids lying and abstains from it. He speaks the truth, is devoted to the truth, reliable, worthy of confidence, not a deceiver of men. Being at a meeting, or amongst people, or in the midst of his relatives, or in a society, or in the king's court, and called upon and asked as witness to tell what he knows, he answers, if he knows nothing: "I know nothing," and if he knows, he answers: "I know"; if he has seen nothing, he answers: "I have seen nothing," and if he has seen, he answers: "I have seen." Thus he never knowingly speaks a lie, either for the sake of his own advantage, or for the sake of another person's advantage, or for the sake of any advantage whatsoever. (AN 10:176)

2. Abstaining from Tale-Bearing

He avoids tale-bearing and abstains from it. What he has heard here, he does not repeat there, so as to cause dissension there; and what he has heard there, he does not repeat here, so as to cause dissension here. Thus he unites those that are divided; and those that are united, he encourages. Concord gladdens him, he delights and rejoices in concord; and it is concord that he spreads by his words.

3. Abstaining from Harsh Language

He avoids harsh language and abstains from it. He speaks such words as are gentle, soothing to the ear, loving, such words as go to the heart and are courteous, friendly, and agreeable to many.

In MN 21, the Buddha says: "Even, O monks, should robbers and murderers saw through your limbs and joints, whosoever should give way to anger because of that would not be following my advice. For thus ought you to train yourselves: 'Undisturbed shall our mind remain, no evil words shall escape our lips; friendly and full of sympathy shall we remain, with heart full of love, and free from any hidden malice; and that person shall we penetrate with loving thoughts, wide, deep, boundless, freed from anger and hatred.'"

4. Abstaining from Vain Talk

He avoids vain talk and abstains from it. He speaks at the right time, in accordance with facts, speaks what is useful, speaks of the Doctrine and the Discipline; his speech is like a treasure, uttered at the right moment, accompanied by arguments, moderate and full of sense.

This is called right speech.

Mundane and Supramundane Right Speech

Now right speech, I tell you, is of two kinds:

1. Abstaining from lying, from tale-bearing, from harsh language, and from vain talk; this is called mundane right speech" (*lokiya sammā-vācā*), which yields worldly fruits and brings good results.

2. But the avoidance of the practice of this fourfold wrong speech, the abstaining, desisting, refraining therefrom—the mind being holy, being turned away from the world, and conjoined with the path, the holy path being pursued—this is called supramundane right speech (*lokuttara sammā-vācā*), which is not of the world, but is supramundane and conjoined with the path.

Conjoined with Other Factors

Now, in understanding wrong speech as wrong, and right speech as right, one practises *right understanding* (1st factor); and in making efforts to overcome wrong speech and to arouse right speech, one practises *right effort* (6th factor); and in overcoming wrong speech with attentive mind, and dwelling with attentive mind in possession of right speech, one practises *right mindfulness* (7th factor). Hence there are three things that accompany and follow upon right speech, namely: right understanding, right effort, and right mindfulness. (MN 117)

Fourth Factor

Right Action

(*sammā-kammanta*)

What now is right action? Abstaining from killing, abstaining from stealing, abstaining from unlawful sexual intercourse. (DN 22)

1. Abstaining From Killing

Herein someone avoids the killing of living beings and abstains from it. Without stick or sword, conscientious, full of sympathy, he is desirous of the welfare of all living beings.

2. Abstaining From Stealing

He avoids stealing and abstains from it; what another person possesses of goods and chattel in the village or in the wood, that he does not take away with thievish intent.

3. Abstaining From Unlawful Sexual Intercourse

He avoids unlawful sexual intercourse and abstains from it. He has no intercourse with such persons as are still under the protection of father, mother, brother, sister or relatives, nor with married women, nor female convicts, nor lastly, with betrothed girls.

This is called right action. (AN 10:176)

MUNDANE AND SUPRAMUNDANE RIGHT ACTION

Now, right action, I tell you, is of two kinds:

1. Abstaining from killing, from stealing, and from unlawful sexual intercourse: this is called mundane right action (*lokiya sammā-kammanta*), which yields worldly fruits and brings good results.

2. But the avoidance of the practice of this threefold wrong action, the abstaining, desisting, refraining therefrom—the mind being holy, being turned away from the world, and conjoined with the path, the holy path being pursued—this is called supramundane right action (*lokuttara sammā-kammanta*), which is not of the world, but is supramundane and conjoined with the path.

CONJOINED WITH OTHER FACTORS

Now, in understanding wrong action as wrong, and right action as right, one practises *right understanding* (1st factor); and in making efforts to overcome wrong action and to arouse right action, one practises *right effort* (6th factor); and in overcoming wrong action with attentive mind, and dwelling with attentive mind in possession of right action, one practises *right mindfulness* (7th factor). Hence, there are three things that accompany and follow upon right action, namely: right understanding, right effort, and right mindfulness. (MN 117)

Fifth Factor

Right Livelihood
(*sammā-ājīva*)

What now is right livelihood? When the noble disciple, avoiding a wrong way of living, earns his livelihood by a right way of living, this is called right livelihood. (DN 22)

In MN 117, it is said: "To practise deceit, treachery, soothsaying, trickery, usury: this is wrong livelihood."

And in AN 5:177, it is said: "Five trades should be avoided by a disciple: trading in arms, in living beings, in flesh, in intoxicating drinks, and in poison."

Included are the professions of a soldier, a fisherman, a hunter, etc.

Mundane and Supramundane Right Livelihood

Now right livelihood, I tell you, is of two kinds:

1. When the noble disciple, avoiding wrong living, gets his livelihood by a right way of living: this is called mundane right livelihood (*lokiya sammā-ājīva*), which yields worldly fruits and brings good results.

2. But the avoidance of wrong livelihood, the abstaining, desisting, refraining therefrom—the mind being holy, being turned away from the world, and conjoined with the path, the holy path being pursued—this is called supramundane right livelihood (*lokuttara sammā-ājīva*), which is not of the world, but is supramundane and conjoined with the path.

Conjoined with Other Factors

Now, in understanding wrong livelihood as wrong, and right livelihood as right, one practises *right understanding* (1st factor); and in making efforts to overcome wrong livelihood, to establish right livelihood, one practises *right effort* (6th factor); and in overcoming wrong livelihood with attentive mind, and dwelling with attentive mind in possession of right livelihood, one practises *right mindfulness* (7th factor). Hence, there are three things that accompany and follow upon right livelihood, namely: right understanding, right effort, and right mindfulness. (MN 117)

Sixth Factor

Right Effort

(sammā-vāyāma)

What now is right effort? There are four great efforts: the effort to avoid, the effort to overcome, the effort to develop, and the effort to maintain.

1. The Effort to Avoid

(saṃvara-padhāna)

What now is the effort to *avoid*? Here the disciple rouses his will to avoid the arising of evil unwholesome states that have not yet arisen; and he makes efforts, stirs up his energy, exerts his mind, and strives.

Thus, when he perceives a form with the eye, a sound with the ear, an odour with the nose, a taste with the tongue, an impression with the body, or an object with the mind, he neither adheres to the whole nor to its parts. And he strives to ward off that through which evil unwholesome states, greed and sorrow, would arise if he remained with unguarded senses; and he watches over his senses, restrains his senses.

Possessed of this noble control over the senses, he experiences inwardly a feeling of joy, into which no evil states can enter.

This is called the effort to avoid.

2. The Effort to Overcome
(*pahāna-padhāna*)

What, now, is the effort to *overcome*? Here the disciple rouses his will to overcome the evil unwholesome states that have already arisen; and he makes effort, stirs up his energy, exerts his mind, and strives.

He does not retain any thought of sensual lust, ill-will, or cruelty, or any other evil unwholesome states that may have arisen; he abandons them, dispels them, destroys them, causes them to disappear. (AN 4:13, 14)

If, while regarding a certain object, there arise in the disciple evil unwholesome thoughts connected with greed, hatred, and delusion, then the disciple (1) should turn away from this object and attend to some other object connected with the wholesome. (2) Or, he should reflect on the misery of these thoughts: "Unwholesome, truly, are these thoughts! Blamable are these thoughts! Of painful result are these thoughts!" (3) Or he should pay no attention to these thoughts. (4) Or he should consider the compound nature of these thoughts. (5) Or, with teeth clenched and tongue pressed against the gums, he should restrain, suppress, and root out these thoughts with his mind; and in doing so these evil unwholesome thoughts of greed, hatred, and delusion will dissolve and disappear; and the mind will inwardly become settled and calm, composed and concentrated.

This is called the effort to overcome. (MN 20)

3. The Effort to Develop
(*bhāvanā-padhāna*)

What, now, is the effort to *develop*? Here the disciple rouses his will to arouse wholesome states that have not yet arisen; and he makes effort, stirs up his energy, exerts his mind, and strives.

Thus he develops the factors of enlightenment (*bojjhaṅga*), based on solitude, on detachment, on extinction, and ending in renunciation, namely: mindfulness (*sati*), investigation of phenomena (*dhamma-vicaya*), energy (*viriya*), rapture (*pīti*), tranquillity (*passaddhi*), concentration (*samādhi*), and equanimity (*upekkhā*).

This is called the effort to develop.

4. The Effort to Maintain
(*anurakkhaṇa-padhāna*)

What, now, is the effort to *maintain*? Here the disciple rouses his will to maintain the wholesome states that have already arisen, and not to allow them to disappear, but to bring them to growth, to maturity, and to the full perfection of development (*bhāvanā*); and he makes effort, stirs up his energy, exerts his mind, and strives.

Thus, for example, he keeps firmly in his mind a favourable object of concentration that has arisen, such as the mental image of a skeleton, of a corpse infested by worms, of a corpse blue-black in colour, of a festering corpse, of a corpse riddled with holes, of a corpse swollen up.

This is called the effort to maintain.

Truly, for a disciple who is possessed of faith and has penetrated the Teaching of the master, it is fit to think: "Though skin, sinews, and bones wither away, though the flesh and blood of my body dry up, I shall not give up my efforts till I have attained whatever is attainable by manly perseverance, energy, and endeavour." (MN 70)

This is called right effort. (AN 4:13, 14)

The effort of avoiding, overcoming,
Of developing and maintaining:
These four great efforts have been shown
By him, the Scion of the Sun.
And one who firmly clings to them,
May put an end to suffering. (AN 6:14)

Seventh Factor

RIGHT MINDFULNESS

(*sammā-sati*)

What now is right mindfulness?

THE FOUR FOUNDATIONS OF MINDFULNESS

(*satipaṭṭhāna*)

The only way that leads to the attainment of purity, to the overcoming of sorrow and lamentation, to the end of pain and grief, to the entering upon the right path and the realization of Nibbāna, is the four foundations of mindfulness. And which are these four?

Here the disciple dwells in contemplation of the body, in contemplation of feeling, in contemplation of the mind, in contemplation of mind-objects, ardent, clearly comprehending them and mindful, after putting away worldly greed and grief.

1. CONTEMPLATION OF THE BODY

(*kāyānupassanā*)

But how does the disciple dwell in contemplation of the body?

Mindfulness of Breathing

(*ānāpāna-sati*)

Here the disciple retires to the forest, to the foot of a tree, or to a solitary place, sits down with legs crossed, body erect, and with mindfulness fixed before him, just mindfully he breathes in, mindfully he breathes out. When making a long inhalation, he knows: "I make a long inhalation"; when making a long exhalation, he knows: "I make a long exhalation." When making a short inhalation, he knows: "I make a short inhalation"; when making a short exhalation, he knows: "I make a short exhalation."

"Clearly perceiving the entire (breath-) body, I shall breathe in": thus he trains himself; "clearly perceiving the entire (breath-) body, I shall breathe out": thus he trains himself. "Calming this bodily function (*kāya-saṅkhāra*), I shall breathe in": thus he trains himself; "calming this bodily function, I shall breathe out": thus he trains himself.

Thus he dwells in contemplation of the body, either with regard to his own person, or to other persons, or to both. He beholds how the body arises; beholds how it passes away; beholds the arising and passing away of the body. A body is there—

> "A body is there, but no living being, no individual, no woman, no man, no self, and nothing that belongs to a self; neither a person, nor anything belonging to a person" (Comy.).

this clear awareness is present in him to the extent necessary for knowledge and mindfulness, and he lives independent, unattached to anything in the world. Thus does the disciple dwell in contemplation of the body.

> "Mindfulness of breathing" (*ānāpāna-sati*) is one of the most important meditative exercises. It may be used for the development of tranquillity (*samatha-bhāvanā*), i.e., for attaining the four absorptions (*jhāna*; see pp. 82–84); for the development of insight (*vipassanā-bhāvanā*); or for a combination of both practices. Here, in the context of *satipaṭṭhāna*, it is principally intended for tranquillization and concentration preparatory to the practice of insight,

which may be undertaken in the following way.

After a certain degree of calm and concentration, or one of the absorptions, has been attained through regular practice of mindful breathing, the disciple proceeds to examine the origin of breath. He sees that the inhalations and exhalations are conditioned by the body consisting of the four material elements and the various corporeal phenomena derived from them, e.g., the five sense organs, etc. Conditioned by fivefold sense-impression arises consciousness, and together with it the three other "groups of existence," i.e., feeling, perception, and mental formations. Thus the meditator sees clearly: "There is no ego-entity or self in this so called personality, but it is only a corporeal and mental process conditioned by various factors." Thereupon he applies the three characteristics to these phenomena, understanding them thoroughly as impermanent, subject to suffering, and non-self.

For further details about *ānāpāna-sati,* see MN 62, MN 118, and Vism VIII.145ff.

The Four Postures

And further, while going, standing, sitting, or lying down, the disciple understands (according to reality) the expressions; "I go"; "I stand"; "I sit"; "I lie down"; he understands any position of the body.

"The disciple understands that there is no living being, no real ego, that goes, stands, etc., but that is by a mere figure of speech that one says: 'I go,' 'I stand,' and so forth" (Comy.).

Mindfulness and Clear Comprehension
(*sati-sampajañña*)

And further, the disciple acts with clear comprehension in going and coming; he acts with clear comprehension in looking forward and backward; acts with clear comprehension in bending and stretching (any part of his body); acts with clear comprehension in carrying his alms bowl and robes; acts with clear comprehension in eating, drinking, chewing, and tasting; acts with clear comprehension in discharging excrement and urine; acts with clear comprehension in walking, standing, sitting, falling asleep, awakening; acts with clear comprehension in speaking and keeping silent.

> "In all that the disciple is doing, he has clear comprehension: (1) of his intention; (2) of his advantage; (3) of his duty; (4) of the reality" (Comy.).

Contemplation of Loathsomeness
(*paṭikkūla-saññā*)

And further, the disciple contemplates this body from the sole of the foot upward, and from the top of the hair downward, with a skin stretched over it, and filled with manifold impurities: "This body has hairs of the head, hairs of the body, nails, teeth, skin, flesh, sinews, bones, marrow, kidneys, heart, liver, diaphragm, spleen, lungs, stomach, bowels, mesentery, and excrement; bile, phlegm, pus, blood, sweat, lymph, tears, skin-grease, saliva, nasal mucus, oil of the joints, and urine."

Just as if there were a sack, with openings at both ends, filled with various kinds of grain—with paddy, beans, sesamum, and husked rice—and a man not blind opened it and examined its contents, thus: "That is paddy, these are beans, this is sesamum, this husked rice"; just so does the disciple investigate this body.

Analysis of Four Elements
(*dhātu*)

And further, the disciple contemplates this body, however it may stand or move, with regard to the elements: "This body consists of the solid element, the liquid element, the heating element, and the vibrating element." Just as if a skilled butcher or a butcher's apprentice, who had slaughtered a cow and divided it into separate portions, were to sit down at the junction of four highroads: just so does the disciple contemplate this body with regard to the elements.

> In Vism XI.30, this simile is explained as follows: When a butcher rears a cow, brings it to the place of slaughter, binds it to a post, makes it stand up, slaughters it and looks at the slaughtered cow, during all that time he has still the notion "cow." But when he has cut up the slaughtered cow, divided it into pieces, and sits down near it to sell the meat, the notion "cow" ceases in his mind, and the notion "meat" arises. He does not think that he is selling a cow or that people buy a cow, but that it is meat that is sold and bought. Similarly, in an ignorant worldling, whether, monk or layman, the concepts "being," "man," "personality," etc., will not cease until he has mentally dissected this body of his, as it stands and moves, and has contemplated it according to its component elements. But when he has done so, the notion "personality," etc., will disappear, and his mind will become firmly established in the contemplation of the elements.

Cemetery Meditations

1. And further, just as if the disciple were looking at a corpse thrown on a charnel ground, one, two, or three days dead, swollen up, blue-black in colour, full of corruption—so he

regards his own body: "This body of mine also has this nature, has this destiny, and cannot escape it."

2. And further, just as if the disciple were looking at a corpse thrown on a charnel ground, eaten by crows, hawks or vultures, by dogs or jackals, or devoured by all kinds of worms, so he regards his own body: "This body of mine also has this nature, has this destiny, and cannot escape it."

3. And further, just as if the disciple were looking at a corpse thrown on a charnel-ground, a framework of bones, flesh hanging from it, bespattered with blood, held together by the sinews …

4. A framework of bone, stripped of flesh, bespattered with blood, held together by the sinews …

5. A framework of bone, without flesh and blood, but still held together by the sinews …

6. Bones, disconnected and scattered in all directions, here a bone of the hand, there a bone of the foot, there a shin bone, there a thigh bone, there a pelvis, there the spine, there the skull—so he regards his own body: "This body of mine also has this nature, has this destiny, and cannot escape it."

7. And further, just as if the disciple were looking at bones lying in the charnel-ground, bleached and resembling shells …

8. Bones heaped together, after the lapse of years …

9. Bones weathered and crumbled to dust, so he regards his own body: "This body of mine also has this nature, has this destiny, and cannot escape it."

Thus he dwells in contemplation of the body, either with regard to his own person, or to other persons, or to both. He beholds how the body arises; beholds how it passes away; beholds the arising and passing away of the body. "A body is there": this clear awareness is present in him to the extent necessary for knowledge and mindfulness; and he lives independent, unattached to anything in the world. Thus does the disciple dwell in contemplation of the body. (DN 22)

Assured of Ten Blessings

Once the contemplation of the body is practised, developed, often repeated, has become one's habit, one's foundation, is firmly established, strengthened, and perfected, the disciple may expect ten blessings.

1. He has mastery over delight and discontent; he is not overcome by discontent; he subdues it as soon as it arises.

2. He conquers fear and anxiety; is not overcome by fear and anxiety; he subdues them as soon as they arise.

3. He endures cold and heat, hunger and thirst, wind and sun, attacks by gadflies, mosquitoes, and reptiles; patiently he endures wicked and malicious speech, as well as bodily pains that befall him, though they be piercing, sharp, bitter, unpleasant, disagreeable, and dangerous to life.

4. He may enjoy at will, without difficulty, without effort, the four absorptions (*jhāna*) which purify the mind and bestow happiness even in this life.

Six Psychical Powers
(*abhiññā*)

5. He may enjoy the different magical powers (*iddhi-vidhā*).

6. With the heavenly ear (*dibba-sota*), purified and superhuman, he may hear both kinds of sounds, the heavenly and the earthly, the distant and the near.

7. With the mind he may obtain insight into the hearts of other beings (*parassa-cetopariya-ñāṇa*), of other persons.

8. He may obtain remembrances of many previous births (*pubbe-nivāsānussati-ñāṇa*).

9. With the heavenly eye (*dibba-cakkhu*), purified and superhuman, he may see beings vanish and reappear, the base

and the noble, the beautiful and the ugly, the happy and the unfortunate; he may perceive how beings are reborn according to their deeds.

10. He may, through the cessation of passions (*āsavakkhaya*), come to know for himself, even in this life, the stainless deliverance of mind, the deliverance through wisdom. (MN 119)

> The last six blessings (5–10) are the psychical powers (*abhiññā*). The first five of them are mundane (*lokiya*) conditions, and may therefore be attained even by a worldling (*puthujjana*), while the last *abhiññā* is supramundane (*lokuttara*) and exclusively the characteristic of the arahant, or Holy One. It is only after the attainment of all the four absorptions (*jhāna*) that one may fully succeed in acquiring the five worldly psychical powers. There are four *iddhipāda*, or "bases for obtaining magical powers," namely: concentration of will, concentration of energy, concentration of mind, and concentration of investigation.

2. Contemplation of Feelings (*vedanānupassanā*)

But how does the disciple dwell in contemplation of feelings?

In experiencing feelings, the disciple knows: "I have an agreeable feeling"; or: "I have a disagreeable feeling," or: "I have an indifferent feeling"; or: "I have a worldly agreeable feeling"; or: "I have an unworldly agreeable feeling"; or: "I have a worldly disagreeable feeling"; or: "I have an unworldly disagreeable feeling"; or: "I have a worldly indifferent feeling"; or: "I have an unworldly indifferent feeling."

Thus he dwells in contemplation of feelings, either with regard to his own person, or to other persons, or to both. He beholds how feelings arise; beholds how they pass away;

beholds the arising and passing away of feelings. "Feelings are there": this clear awareness is present in him to the extent necessary for knowledge and mindfulness; and he lives independent, unattached to anything in the world. Thus does the disciple dwell in contemplation of feelings.

> The disciple understands that the expression "I feel" has no validity except as a conventional expression (*vohāra-vacana*); he understand that, in the absolute sense (*paramattha*), there are only feelings, and that there is no self, no experiencer of feelings.

3. Contemplation of the Mind
(*cittānupassanā*)

But how does the disciple dwell in contemplation of the mind?

Here the disciple knows the greedy mind as greedy, and the not greedy mind as not greedy; knows the hating mind as hating, and the not hating mind as not hating: knows the deluded mind as deluded, and the undeluded mind as undeluded. He knows the cramped mind as cramped, and the scattered mind as scattered; knows the developed mind as developed, and the undeveloped mind as undeveloped; knows the surpassable mind as surpassable, and the unsurpassable mind as unsurpassable; knows the concentrated mind as concentrated, and the unconcentrated mind as unconcentrated; knows the freed mind as freed, and the unfreed mind as unfreed.

> *Citta* (mind) is here used as a collective term for the *cittas*, or moments of consciousness. *Citta,* being identical with *viññāṇa* or consciousness, should not be translated by "thought." "Thought" and "thinking" correspond rather to the "verbal operations of the mind"—*vitakka* (thought-conception) and *vicāra* (discursive thinking), which belong to the *saṅkhārakkhandha*.

Thus he dwells in contemplation of the mind, either with regard to his own person, or to other persons, or to both. He beholds how mind arises; beholds how it passes away; beholds the arising and passing away of mind. "Mind is there": this clear awareness is present in him to the extent necessary for knowledge and mindfulness; and he lives independent, unattached to anything in the world. Thus does the disciple dwell in contemplation of the mind.

4. Contemplation of Mind-Objects
(*dhammānupassanā*)

But how does the disciple dwell in contemplation of mind-objects?

Herein the disciple dwells in contemplation of mind-objects, namely, of the five hindrances.

The Five Hindrances
(*pañca nīvaraṇa*)

1. He knows when there is lust (*kāmacchanda*) in him: "There is lust in me"; knows when there is anger (*vyāpāda*) in him: "There is anger in me"; knows when there is torpor and sloth (*thīna-middha*) in him: "There is torpor and sloth in me"; knows when there is restlessness and mental worry (*uddhacca-kukkucca*) in him: "There is restlessness and mental worry in me"; knows when there is doubt (*vicikicchā*) in him: "There is doubt in me." He knows when these hindrances are absent in him: "These hindrances are absent in me." He knows how they come to arise; he knows how, once arisen, they are overcome; and he knows how they do not arise again in the future.

For example, lust arises through unwise thinking on the agreeable and delightful. It may be suppressed by the following six methods: fixing the mind upon an idea that arouses disgust; contemplation of the loathsomeness of the body; controlling one's six senses; moderation in eating; friendship with wise and good people; right instruction. Lust and anger are permanently extinguished upon attainment of non-returning (*anāgāmitā*) restlessness is extinguished by reaching arahantship; mental worry, by reaching stream-entry (*sotāpatti*).

The Five Groups of Existence (*pañcakhandha*)

And further: the disciple dwells in contemplation of mind-objects, namely, of the five groups of existence. He knows what corporeality (*rūpa*) is, how it arises, how it passes away; he knows what feeling (*vedanā*) is, how it arises, how it passes away; knows what perception (*saññā*) is, how it arises, how it passes away; he knows what the mental formations (*saṅkhārā*) are, how they arise, how they pass away; he knows what consciousness (*viññāṇa*) is, how it arises, how it passes away.

The Sense-Bases (*Saḷāyatana*)

And further: the disciple dwells in contemplation of mind-objects, namely, of the six subjective and objective sense-bases. He knows the eye and visual objects, ear and sounds, nose and odours, tongue and tastes, body and bodily impressions, mind and mind-objects; and he also knows the fetter that arises in dependence on them. He knows how the fetter comes to arise; he knows how the fetter is overcome; and he knows how the abandoned fetter does not arise again in the future.

The Seven Factors of Enlightenment
(*satta bojjhaṅgā*)

And further: the disciple dwells in contemplation of mind-objects, namely, of the seven factors of enlightenment. He knows when there is in him mindfulness (*sati*), investigation of phenomena (*dhammavicaya*), energy (*viriya*), rapture (*pīti*), tranquillity (*passaddhi*), concentration (*samādhi*), and equanimity (*upekkhā*). He knows when they are not in him; he knows how they come to arise; he knows how they are fully developed.

The Four Noble Truths
(*cattāri ariya-saccāni*)

And further: the disciple dwells in contemplation of mind-objects, namely, of the Four Noble Truths. He knows according to reality what suffering is; he knows according to reality what the origin of suffering is; he knows according to reality what the extinction of suffering is; he knows according to reality what the path is that leads to the extinction of suffering.

Thus he dwells in contemplation of mind-objects either with regard to his own person, or to other persons, or to both. He beholds how the mind-objects arise, beholds how they pass away, beholds the arising and passing away of the mind-objects. "Mind-objects are there": this clear awareness is present in him to the extent necessary for knowledge and mindfulness; and he lives independent, unattached to anything in the world. Thus does the disciple dwell in contemplation of the mind-objects.

The only way that leads to the attainment of purity, to the overcoming of sorrow and lamentation, to the end of pain and grief, to the entering upon the right path and the realization of Nibbāna, is by these four foundations of mindfulness. (DN 22)

These four contemplations of *satipaṭṭhāna* relate to all the five groups of existence, namely: (1) the contemplation of body relates to the aggregate of corporeality; (2) the contemplation of feeling, to the aggregate of feeling; (3) the contemplation of mind, to the aggregate of consciousness; (4) the contemplation of mind-objects, to the aggregates of perception and mental formations.

For further details about *satipaṭṭhāna*, see the commentary to the discourse of that name, translated in *The Way of Mindfulness*, by Bhikkhu Soma (Buddhist Publication Society).

Nibbāna through Ānāpāna-Sati

Mindfulness of in-and-out breathing (*ānāpāna-sati*), practised and developed, brings the four foundations of mindfulness to perfection; the four foundations of mindfulness, practised and developed, bring the seven factors of enlightenment to perfection; the seven factors of enlightenment, practised and developed, bring wisdom and deliverance to perfection.

But how does mindfulness of in-and-out breathing, practised and developed, bring the four foundations of mindfulness to perfection?

I. Whenever the disciple (1) mindfully makes a long inhalation or exhalation, or (2) makes a short inhalation or exhalation, or (3) trains himself to inhale or exhale while experiencing the whole (breath-) body, or (4) calms down this bodily function (i.e., the breath)—at such a time the disciple dwells in contemplation of the body, full of energy, comprehending it, mindful, after subduing worldly greed and grief. For I call inhalation and exhalation one among the corporeal phenomena.

II. Whenever the disciple trains himself to inhale or exhale (1) while feeling rapture (*pīti*), or (2) joy (*sukha*), or (3) the mental functions (*cittasaṅkhāra*), or (4) while calming down the mental functions—at such a time he dwells in contemplation of feelings, full of energy, clearly comprehending them, mindful, after subduing worldly greed and grief. For I call the full awareness of in-and-out breathing one among the feelings.

III. Whenever the disciple trains himself to inhale or exhale (1) while experiencing the mind, or (2) while gladdening the mind, or (3) while concentrating the mind, or (4) while setting the mind free—at such a time he dwells in contemplation of the mind, full of energy, clearly comprehending it, mindful, after subduing worldly greed and grief. For without mindfulness and clear comprehension, I say, there is no mindfulness of in-and-out breathing.

IV. Whenever the disciple trains himself to inhale or exhale while contemplating (1) impermanence, or (2) the fading away of passion, or (3) extinction, or (4) detachment—at such a time he dwells in contemplation of mind-objects, full of energy, clearly comprehending them, mindful, after subduing worldly greed and grief. Having seen, through understanding, what is the abandoning of greed and grief, he looks on with complete equanimity.

Mindfulness of in-and-out breathing, thus practised and developed, brings the four foundations of mindfulness to perfection.

But how do the four foundations of mindfulness, practised and developed, bring the seven factors of enlightenment to full perfection?

1. Whenever the disciple dwells in contemplation of body, feelings, mind, and mind-objects, strenuous, clearly comprehending them, mindful, after subduing worldly greed and grief—at such a time his mindfulness is undisturbed; and whenever his mindfulness is present and undisturbed, at such a time he has gained and develops the factor of

enlightenment mindfulness (*sati-sambojjhaṅga*); and thus this factor of enlightenment reaches fullest perfection.

2. And whenever, while dwelling with mindfulness, he wisely investigates, examines, and thinks over the doctrine (*dhamma*)—at such a time he has gained and develops the factor of enlightenment investigation of phenomena (*dhamma-vicaya-sambojjhaṅga*); and thus this factor of enlightenment reaches fullest perfection.

3. And whenever, while wisely investigating, examining, and thinking over the doctrine, his energy is firm and unshaken—at such a time he has gained and develops the factor of enlightenment energy (*viriya-sambojjhaṅga*); and thus this factor of enlightenment reaches fullest perfection.

4. And whenever, while he is firm in energy, super-sensuous rapture arises in him—at such a time he has gained and develops the factor of enlightenment rapture (*pīti-sambojjhaṅga*); and thus this factor of enlightenment reaches fullest perfection.

5. And whenever, while enraptured in mind, his spiritual frame and his mind become tranquil—at such a time he has gained and develops the factor of enlightenment tranquillity (*passaddhi-sambojjhaṅga*); and thus this factor of enlightenment reaches fullest perfection.

6. And whenever, while being tranquillized in his spiritual frame and happy, his mind becomes concentrated—at such a time he has gained and develops the factor of enlightenment concentration (*samādhi-sambojjhaṅga*); and thus this factor of enlightenment reaches fullest perfection.

7. And whenever he looks with complete indifference on his mind thus concentrated—at such a time he has gained and develops the factor of enlightenment equanimity (*upekkhā-sambojjhaṅga*); and thus this factor of enlightenment reaches fullest perfection.

The four foundations of mindfulness, thus practised and developed, bring the seven factors of enlightenment to full perfection.

And how do the seven factors of enlightenment, practised and developed, bring wisdom and deliverance (*vijjā-vimutti*) to full perfection?

Here the disciple develops the factors of enlightenment: mindfulness, investigation of phenomena, energy, rapture, tranquillity, concentration, and equanimity, based on detachment, on absence of desire, on extinction, ending in renunciation.

The seven factors of enlightenment, thus practised and developed, bring wisdom and deliverance to full perfection.

(MN 118)

Just as the elephant hunter drives a huge stake into the ground and chains the wild elephant to it by the neck, in order to drive out of him his habitual forest ways and wishes, his forest unruliness, obstinacy, and violence, and to accustom him to the environment of the village, and to teach him such good behaviour as is required among men; in like manner also the noble disciple should fix his mind firmly to these four foundations of mindfulness, so that he may drive out of himself his habitual worldly ways and wishes, his habitual worldly unruliness, obstinacy, and violence, and enter upon the right path and realize Nibbāna. (MN 125)

Eighth Factor

Right Concentration
(*sammā-samādhi*)

What now is right concentration?

Its Definition

Having the mind fixed to a single object (*cittekaggatā*, lit. "one-pointedness of mind"): this is concentration.

Its Objects

The four foundations of mindfulness (7th factor): these are the objects of concentration.

Its Requisites

The four great efforts (6th factor): these are the requisites for concentration.

Its Development

The practising, developing, and cultivating of these things: this is the development (*bhāvanā*) of concentration. (MN 44)

> Right concentration has two degrees of development: (1) "neighbourhood concentration" (*upacāra-samādhi*), which approaches the first absorption without, however, attaining it; (2) "attainment concentration" (*appanā-samādhi*), which is the concentration present in the four absorptions (*jhāna*). These absorptions are mental states beyond the reach of the fivefold sense-activity, attainable only in solitude and by unremitting perseverence in the practice of concentration. In these states all activity of

the five senses is suspended. No visual or audible impressions arise at such a time, no bodily feeling is felt. But although all outer sense-impressions have ceased, the mind remains active, perfectly alert, fully awake.

The attainment of these absorptions, however, is not a requisite for the realization of the four supramundane paths of holiness; and neither neighbourhood concentration nor attainment concentration, as such, possesses the power of conferring entry to the four supramundane paths; hence they really have no power to free one permanently from evil things. The realization of the four supramundane paths is possible only at the moment of deep insight (*vipassanā*) into the impermanency (*aniccatā*), suffering (*dukkhatā*), and selfless nature (*anattatā*) of this whole phenomenal process of existence. This insight, again, is attainable only during neighbourhood concentration, not during attainment concentration.

One who has realized one or other of the four supramundane paths, without ever having attained the absorptions, is called *sukkha-vipassaka*, or *suddhavipassanā-yānika*, i.e., "one who has taken merely insight (*vipassanā*) as his vehicle (*yāna*)". One, however, who has reached one of the supramundane paths after cultivating the absorptions, is called *samathayānika*, or "one who has taken tranquillity (*samatha*) as his vehicle (*yāna*)."

For *samatha* and *vipassanā*, see Fund. IV and B. Dict.

THE FOUR ABSORPTIONS
(*jhāna*)

Detached from sensual pleasures, detached from evil states, the disciple enters into the first absorption, which is accompanied by thought conception and discursive thinking, is born of detachment, and filled with rapture and happiness. (DN 22)

> This is the first of the absorptions belonging to the fine-material sphere (*rūpāvacarajjhāna*). It is attained when, through the strength of concentration, the fivefold sense activity is temporarily suspended, and the five hindrances are likewise eliminated.
>
> See B. Dict.: *kasiṇa, nimitta, samādhi.*

This first absorption is free from five things, and five things are present. When the disciple enters the first absorption, there have vanished (the five hindrances): lust, ill-will, torpor and sloth, restlessness and worry, and doubt; and there are present: thought-conception (*vitakka*), discursive thinking (*vicāra*), rapture (*pīti*), happiness (*sukha*), and concentration (*citt'ekaggatā = samādhi*).

> These five mental factors present in the first absorption are called factors (or constituents) of absorption (*jhānaṅga*). *Vitakka* (initial formation of an abstract thought) and *vicāra* (discursive thinking, rumination) are called "verbal functions" (*vaci-saṅkhāra*) of the mind; hence they are something secondary to consciousness. In the *Visuddhimagga*, *vitakka* is compared to the taking hold of a pot, and *vicāra* to the wiping of it. In the first absorption both are present, but are exclusively focussed on the subject of meditation; *vicāra* is here not discursive, but of an "exploring" nature. Both are entirely absent in the following absorptions.

And further: after the subsiding of thought-conception and discursive thinking, and by the gaining of inner tranquillity and oneness of mind, he enters into a state free from thought-conception and discursive thinking, the second absorption, which is born of concentration (*samādhi*), and filled with rapture (*pīti*) and happiness (*sukha*).

> In the second absorption, there are three factors of absorption: rapture, happiness, and concentration.

And further: after the fading away of rapture, he dwells in equanimity, mindful, with clear awareness: and he experiences in his own person that feeling of which the noble ones say: "Happy lives he who is equanimous and mindful." Thus he enters the third absorption.

> In the third absorption there are two factors of absorption: equanimous happiness (*upekkhā-sukha*) and concentration (*citt'ekaggatā*).

And further: after the giving up of pleasure and pain, and through the disappearance of previous joy and grief, he enters into a state beyond pleasure and pain, into the fourth absorption, which is purified by equanimity and mindfulness. (MN 43)

> In the fourth absorption there are two factors of absorption: concentration and equanimity (*upekkhā*).
>
> In the *Visuddhimagga* forty subjects of meditation (*kammaṭṭhāna*) are enumerated and treated in detail. By their successful practice the following absorptions may be attained.
>
> All four absorptions: through mindfulness of breathing (see Vism VIII.145ff.), the ten kasiṇa-exercises (Vism IV, V, and B. Dict.); the contemplation of equanimity (*upekkhā*), being the practice of the fourth *brahma-vihāra* (Vism IX.88–90).
>
> The first three absorptions: through the development of loving-kindness (*mettā*), compassion (*karuṇā*), and sympathetic joy (*muditā*), being the practice of the first three *brahma-vihāras* (Vism IX.1ff.).
>
> The first absorption: through the ten contemplations

of impurity (*asubha-bhāvanā;* i.e., the cemetery contemplations, which are ten according to the enumeration in Vism VI); the contemplation of the body (i.e., the thirty-two parts of the body; see Vism VIII.42ff.).

"Neighbourhood-concentration" (*upacāra-samādhi*): through the recollections on the Buddha, Dhamma, and Sangha, on morality, liberality, heavenly beings, peace (= Nibbāna), and death (Vism VII, VIII.1ff.); the contemplation on the loathsomeness of food (Vism XI.1ff.); the analysis of the four elements (Vism XI.27ff.).

The four immaterial absorptions (*arūpa-jhāna* or *āruppa*), which are based on the fourth absorption, are produced by meditating on their respective objects from which they derive their names: the spheres of unbounded space, of unbounded consciousness, of nothingness, and of neither-perception-nor-non-perception (Vism X).

All the objects and methods of concentration are treated in Vism III–XIII; see also Fund. IV.

Develop your concentration; for one who has concentration understands things according to reality. And what are these things? The arising and passing away of corporeality, feeling, perception, mental formations, and consciousness. (SN 22:5)

Thus these five groups of existence must be wisely penetrated; ignorance and craving must be wisely abandoned; tranquillity (*samatha*) and insight (*vipassanā*) must be wisely developed. (MN 149)

This is the Middle Path which the Perfect One has discovered, which makes one both to see and to know, and which leads to peace, to discernment, to enlightenment, to Nibbāna. (SN 56:11)

And following this path,
You will put an end to suffering. (Dhp 275)

Gradual Development of the Eightfold Path in the Progress of the Disciple

Confidence and Right Thought
(Second Factor)

Suppose a householder, or his son, or someone reborn in a good family, hears the Doctrine; and after hearing the Doctrine he is filled with confidence in the Perfect One. And filled with this confidence, he thinks: "Full of hindrances is household life, a refuse heap; but the homeless life (of a monk) is like the open air. Not easy is it, when one lives at home, to fulfil in all points the rules of the holy life. Let me now cut off hair and beard, put on the yellow robe, and go forth from home to the homeless life." And in a short time, having given up his possessions, great or little, having forsaken a large or small circle of relations, he cuts off hair and beard, puts on the yellow robe, and goes forth from home to the homeless life.

Morality
(Third, Fourth, Fifth Factors)

Having thus left the world, he fulfils the rules of the monks. He avoids the killing of living beings and abstains from it. Without stick or sword, conscientious, full of sympathy, he is desirous of the welfare of all living beings. He avoids stealing, and abstains from taking what is not given to him. He takes only what is given to him, waiting till it is given; and he lives with a heart honest and pure. He avoids unchastity, living chaste, celibate, and aloof from the vulgar practice of sexual intercourse.

He avoids lying and abstains from it. He speaks the truth, is devoted to the truth, reliable, worthy of confidence, no deceiver of people. He avoids tale-bearing and abstains from it. What he has heard here, he does not repeat there, so as to cause dissension there; and what he has heard there, he does not repeat here, so as to cause dissension here. Thus he unites those that are divided, and those that are united he encourages; concord gladdens him, he delights and rejoices in concord; and it is concord that he spreads by his words. He avoids harsh language and abstains from it. He speaks such words as are gentle, soothing to the ear, loving, such words as go to the heart, and are courteous, friendly, and agreeable to many. He avoids vain talk and abstains from it. He speaks at the right time, in accordance with facts, speaks what is useful, speaks of the Doctrine and the Discipline; his speech is like a treasure, uttered at the right moment, accompanied by arguments, moderate and full of sense.

He takes food only at one time of the day (forenoon), abstains from food in the evening, does not eat at improper times. He keeps aloof from dance, song, music, and the visiting of shows; he rejects flowers, perfumes, ointment, as well as every kind of adornment and embellishment. High and gorgeous beds he does not use. Gold and silver he does not accept. He does not accept raw corn and flesh, women and girls, male and female slaves, or goats, sheep, fowls, pigs, elephants, cows or horses, or land and goods. He does not go on errands and do the duties of a messenger. He eschews buying and selling things. He has nothing to do with false measures, metals, and weights. He avoids the crooked ways of bribery, deception, and fraud. He has no part in stabbing, beating, chaining, attacking, plundering, and oppressing.

He contents himself with the robe that protects his body, and with the almsbowl by means of which he keeps himself alive. Wherever he goes, he is provided with these two things, just as a winged bird in flying carries his wings along with him. By fulfilling this noble domain of morality (*sīlakkhandha*) he feels in his heart an irreproachable happiness.

CONTROL OF THE SENSES
(SIXTH FACTOR)

Now, in perceiving a form with the eye ... a sound with the ear ... an odour with the nose ... a taste with the tongue ... an impression with the body ... an object with the mind, he cleaves neither to the whole nor to its details. And he tries to ward off that which, should he be unguarded in his senses, might give rise to evil and unwholesome states, to greed and sorrow; he watches over his senses, keeps his senses under control. By practising this noble control of the senses (*indriya-saṃvara*), he feels in his heart an unblemished happiness.

MINDFULNESS AND CLEAR COMPREHENSION
(SEVENTH FACTOR)

He is mindful and acts with clear comprehension when going and coming; when looking forward and backward; when bending and stretching his limbs; when wearing his robes and carrying his almsbowl; when eating, drinking, chewing, and tasting; when discharging excrement and urine; when walking, standing, sitting, falling asleep, and awakening; when speaking and keeping silent.

Now being equipped with this noble morality (*sīla*), equipped with this noble control of the senses (*indriya-saṃvara*), and filled with this noble mindfulness and clear comprehension (*sati-sampajañña*), he chooses a secluded dwelling in the forest, at the foot of a tree, on a mountain, in a cleft, in a rock cave, on a burial ground, on a wooded table-land, in the open air, or on a heap of straw. Having returned from his alms round, after the meal he sits down with legs crossed, body erect, with mindfulness fixed before him.

Abandoning the Five Hindrances

He has cast away lust (*kāmacchanda*); he dwells with a heart free from lust; he cleanses his heart from lust.

He has cast away ill-will (*vyāpāda*); he dwells with a heart free from ill-will; cherishing love and compassion toward all living beings, he cleanses his heart from ill-will.

He has cast away torpor and sloth (*thīnamiddha*); he dwells free from torpor and sloth; loving the light, with watchful mind, with clear comprehension, he cleanses his mind from torpor and sloth.

He has cast away restlessness and worry (*uddhacca-kukkucca*); dwelling with mind undisturbed, with heart full of peace, he cleanses his mind from restlessness and worry.

He has cast away doubt (*vicikicchā*); dwelling free from doubt, full of confidence in the good, he cleanses his heart from doubt.

The Absorptions
(Eighth Factor)

He has put aside these five hindrances, the corruptions of the mind that paralyse wisdom. Detached from sensual pleasures, detached from evil states, he enters into the four absorptions (*jhāna*). (MN 38)

Insight
(First Factor)

But whatsoever there is of corporeality, feeling, perception, mental formations, or consciousness, all these phenomena he regards as impermanent (*anicca*), subject to pain (*dukkha*), as infirm, as an ulcer, a thorn, a misery, a burden, an enemy, a disturbance, as empty, and not self (*anattā*); and turning away from these things, he directs his mind towards the Deathless thus: "This, truly, is peace, this is the highest, namely, the end of all karma-formations, the forsaking of every substratum of rebirth, the fading away of craving, detachment, extinction, Nibbāna." And in this state he reaches the cessation of passions (*āsavakkhaya*). (AN 9:36)

Nibbāna

And his heart becomes free from sensual passion (*kāmāsava*), free from the passion for existence (*bhavāsava*), free from the passion of ignorance (*avijjāsava*). "Freed am I!"—this knowledge arises in the liberated one; and he knows: "Exhausted is rebirth; fulfilled the holy life; what had to be done has been done; nothing more remains for this world." (MN 39)

Forever am I liberated,
This is the last time that I'm born,
No new existence waits for me. (MN 26)

This is, indeed, the highest, holiest peace: appeasement of greed, hatred, and delusion.

The Silent Thinker

"I am" is a vain thought; "I am this" is a vain thought; "I shall be" is a vain thought; "I shall not be" is a vain thought. Vain thoughts are a sickness, an ulcer, a thorn. But after overcoming all vain thoughts, one is called a silent thinker. And the thinker, the Silent One, does no more arise, no more pass away, no more tremble, no more desire. For there is nothing in him whereby he should arise again. And as he arises no more, how should he grow old again? And as he grows old no more, how should he die again? And as he dies no more, how should he tremble? And as he trembles no more, how should he have desire? (MN 140)

The True Goal

Hence the purpose of the holy life does not consist in acquiring wealth, honour, or fame, nor in gaining morality, concentration, or the eye of knowledge. That unshakable deliverance of the heart: that, indeed, is the object of the holy life, that is its essence, that is its goal. (MN 29)

And those who in the past were Holy and Enlightened Ones, those Blessed Ones too have pointed out to their disciples this self-same goal as has been pointed out by me to my disciples. And those who in the future will be Holy and Enlightened Ones, those Blessed Ones too will point out to their disciples this self-same goal as has been pointed out by me to my disciples. (MN 51)

However, disciples, it may be that after my passing away you might think: "Gone is the doctrine of our master. We have no master anymore." But you should not think thus; for the Doctrine (*dhamma*) and the Discipline (*vinaya*) that I have taught you will be your master after my death.

Let the Doctrine be your isle!
Let the Doctrine be your refuge!
Look for no other refuge!

Therefore, disciples, the doctrines that I taught you after having penetrated them myself, you should well preserve, well guard, so that this holy life may take its course and continue for ages, for the good and welfare of the many, as a consolation to the world, for the happiness, good, and welfare of heavenly beings and humans. (DN 16)

Of related interest

The Buddha's Path to Deliverance

Nyanatiloka Mahāthera

Larger in size and more advanced in treatment than *The Word of the Buddha*, this book arranges the Buddha's discourses into the threefold framework of morality, concentration, and wisdom, and the seven stages of purity.

BP 202S, Publ. 2010 202 pp.

Buddhist Dictionary

Nyanatiloka Mahāthera

Authentic, clear explanations of all key Theravada Buddhist terms and doctrines, arranged alphabetically, with textual references. An indispensable aid for the serious student of Theravada Buddhism.

BP 601S, Publ. 2004 272 pp.

The Life of Nyanatiloka Thera

The Biography of a Western Buddhist Pioneer

Ordained as one of the first Western monks in 1903, Nyanatiloka was an influential Western Buddhist pioneer. This book consists of a translation of Nyanatiloka's autobiography of the first part of his adventurous life, followed by a biographical postscript drawn from other sources.

BP 604S, Publ. 2008 274 pp.

THE BUDDHIST PUBLICATION SOCIETY

The BPS is an approved charity dedicated to making known the Teaching of the Buddha, which has a vital message for all people.

Founded in 1958, the BPS has published a wide variety of books and booklets covering a great range of topics. Its publications include accurate annotated translations of the Buddha's discourses, standard reference works, as well as original contemporary expositions of Buddhist thought and practice. These works present Buddhism as it truly is—a dynamic force which has influenced receptive minds for the past 2500 years and is still as relevant today as it was when it first arose.

For more information about the BPS and our publications, please visit our website, or write an e-mail, or a letter to the:

Administrative Secretary
Buddhist Publication Society
P.O. Box 61
54 Sangharaja Mawatha
Kandy • Sri Lanka
E-mail: bps@bps.lk
web site: http://www.bps.lk
Tel: 0094 81 223 7283 • Fax: 0094 81 222 3679